FINDING AZTEC GOLD

To Colleen
Find Your Gold!
Miki Banavige

A GIFT TO ALL THOSE OVER FIFTY
& THE MANY LIVES THEY TOUCH

Miki Banavige

Goblin Fern Press

Madison, Wisconsin

ISBN: 1-59598-021-0

LCCN: 2004114789

Published by:
Goblin Fern Press, Inc.
3809 Mineral Point Road
Madison, WI 53705
www.goblinfernpress.com

Cover artwork by Wendy J. Johnson, Elder Eye Design
Book design and production: Goblin Fern Press

Printed in the United States of America
First printing

Dedication

To Jan Tillotson,
Life Coach and Friend Forever,
you believed in this book from the
very beginning

and

To my Grandchildren:
Ben, Jeb, Maeve and Ronan...
follow your dreams and
you will soar to great heights

Prologue

The basis for this book originally began in my head and then ultimately became a reality, a self fulfilling prophesy even better than what I had created in my own mind. It has always been said that truth is stranger than fiction. The story centers around four ordinary "prime-time" women from Minnesota on a two week adventure to Mexico in search of the migrating Monarch butterflies. There are actually three threads to follow running through each chapter. The first, our personal stories which are true except for a little literary license taken here and there. The second, the gifts of wisdom from our wise guide, Manuel, which are half true and half fiction. The third thread is a melding of what we actually encountered and experienced day to day, which is once again true except for a little rearranging and literary license. The historical facts and legends are accurate and were confirmed by my reading and research.

When we set out for Mexico, I was age sixty, mother of two and grandmother of three, divorced, and had worked throughout the years as an executive director of the Wayzata Chamber of Commerce, as a food writer, cooking instructor, cookbook author and in retail sales. Jo Ann, age fifty-eight, married, mother of two and grandmother of four, had also worked as an executive director of the Wayzata Chamber of Commerce, in banking and for a travel agency in Wayzata. Beryl Marie, age sixty-one, widowed, mother of six and grandmother of three, had worked as a teacher, tutor and day care provider. Adrienne, age fifty-nine, married, mother of two and grandmother of three, had worked as a nurse, in incentive merchandise sales, and had started and eventually sold the Wayzata Quilting Emporium.

Throughout my life, I have spent many happy hours reading both fiction and non-fiction, and participating in book discussion groups, and so I have attempted to write a book that I, myself, would love to read and discuss. Enjoy!

— Miki Banavige

Minneapolis

Just like a robot, I moved through the motions of getting out of bed and getting dressed. Later that morning I would stand before the judge to dissolve my marriage to Dan, my husband of thirty years. A marriage of thirty years took less than thirty minutes to end legally, surprisingly less time than the marriage ceremony and celebration itself. It was this plus all the years of conflict leading up to the divorce that made me feel so numb now. We never did agree on much of what was worthwhile in life. One of our many arguments had been around travel. While travel was not at all important to Dan, my greatest wish was to see the world. When I returned from court, I stood on my deck, shattered but relieved. It was a sparkling September day and I watched the playful Monarch butterflies as they flitted with purpose from flower to flower in my garden, finally soaring freely and effortlessly toward Mexico. I studied them with great interest, hoping that one day soon, I could do the same.

Jo Ann and I had met on several community volunteer projects. Today she stood in a field of fall wildflowers with a net, catching, tagging and releasing Monarch butterflies to be identified later by other volunteers in Mexico, where the butterflies migrated to their winter home. This warm and wonderful late September day was a special bonus before the long, cold Minnesota winter ahead. As Jo Ann enjoyed the soothing warmth of the sun on her skin, she wondered why she had always been so magnetically drawn to Monarch butterflies. Perhaps it was because the butterfly had always been the unofficial symbol for Al-Anon. Her husband, Don, had long ago discovered the benefits of belonging to Alcoholics Anonymous, yet he chose not to remain anonymous to better help others. Jo Ann had found and given support through the years by faithfully attending Al-Anon, the group created especially for families and friends of alcoholics.

When the phone rang on that October morning, my future friend Beryl wasn't going to answer. She was busy preparing for a trip she would be taking with her husband, Jerry, later that week. Her thoughts were on how much she loved it when Jerry, even at the age of fifty-five, sometimes sang silly little Spanish love songs to her, learned during his college travels in Mexico. She did, however, finally answer the relentless ring and was gently told that Jerry would not be coming home again, ever. He had just suffered a massive heart attack at work.

As Beryl hung up the phone, the one thing she remembered was a lone Monarch butterfly outside her window, gracefully heading toward heaven. Once the shock wore off, she realized it was now only her who was left to look after herself and her six children.

It was a picture-perfect Thanksgiving Day in Minnesota, when suddenly, Adrienne, my acquaintance of many years, found herself lying on the side of the road, surrounded by snow. She had just been hit by a car while taking a quick walk with her husband, Jack, before their big family dinner. Unconscious, her injured brain focused on the Day of the Dead celebration she had witnessed in Mexico just a few weeks earlier. Surreal dancing skeletons now invited her to join them and let her soul take flight with the swarms of other Monarch butterflies, for Mexicans believe migrating Monarchs are the returning souls of their departed loved ones. Adrienne kept fighting off the stubborn skeletons and continued trying to regain consciousness. She loved her life and her family, and they needed her. She was by no means ready to join the dead.

More than half a dozen years had passed since those events. Was it fate, then, that brought the four of us together one very ordinary fall morning at Lake Country Coffee? We were all simply on our way to work or to do errands, and had stopped for our daily dose of caffeine. Our gods were certainly working overtime to make sure that we crossed paths and connected that morning. We had been mere acquaintances in the community throughout the years, but when we began casually chatting over coffee, we somehow discovered that each had a strong interest in Mexico and a special desire to follow the migration of the Monarchs. We also discovered that in our recent pasts, each had faced and survived a major set-back in her life. We were now ready to shed our cocoons of crisis. One year later, our dream to see the butterflies would become reality.

Mexico City

Looking over the waiting crowd, we couldn't miss the face of our guide. His infectious grin lit up the whole room with the warmth and intensity of the mid-day Mexican sun. For the next two weeks, Manuel would lead us on an amazing adventure throughout central Mexico. Here we were, four fun-loving, middle-aged, middle-American women who had just landed at the Mexico City Airport on that January day at the turn of the millennium. Brought together as acquaintances, we would become bonded as friends by what we would discover on this trip. Now we were all free and ready to soar, just like the wintering Monarchs we had come to see. The snow and cold and family restrictions of Minnesota were quickly forgotten after our first margarita.

We deeply wanted to experience all that central Mexico had to offer, but actually making the trip had taken a lot of courage. Our well-meaning families and friends warned us that unless we were extremely careful, we could easily be robbed, raped, drugged, killed, kidnapped, or get sick from the food, water, smog or high altitude. The media and official travel alerts had also pointed out that we were subject to possible civil or political uprisings and natural disasters such as earthquakes, volcanic eruptions and wild forest fires. Hey, we had just successfully survived Y2K. Given that, we had all said: "Let's go!"

Manuel quickly gathered us together and loaded our luggage into his van for the short ride to Cuernavaca. This "city of eternal spring" would be our headquarters for the entire trip. As we made the journey through the mountains, we began an even more fascinating journey into the personality of our guide. We learned that Manuel was many men in one: architect, professor, philosopher, healer, ecologist and humanitarian. Besides speaking excellent English, he was gentle yet strong, well-weathered and over fifty, just like us. He shared our passion for travel, and we were certainly fortunate to have someone of his caliber leading and protecting us.

Our first brief lesson would be about Mexico and our surroundings. Manuel explained that his country had been described as a "cornucopia of contrasts." Ancient pyramids stand next to colonial churches and modern skyscrapers. The diverse landscape consists of mountains, plains, deserts, jungles and ocean beaches. The people themselves are also a study in contrasts, combining Indian and Spanish blood, as well as Catholic and native traditions even to this day. The mighty Aztecs were conquered by the Spanish in the early fifteen-hundreds and lived under Spanish rule for exactly three centuries. After a long and painful revolution, Mexico finally won its independence from Spain in 1821. Modern-day Mexico offers hidden meaning at every turn. As we were soon to find out, nothing in Mexico is as it appears.

Arriving in Cuernavaca, our first errand was to stop at the bank and change dollars into pesos. We were emphatically reminded that we constantly needed to keep our guard up regarding our personal safety and well-being. Manuel pointed out that it was obvious to any onlooker that we now had large sums of pesos, so one of the armed bank guards escorted us back to the van and saw us securely locked in and on our way, while watching to ensure that no one was rushing to a car to follow us.

The next stop was the grocery store. There we stocked up for several days and Manuel, with great charm and patience, helped us communicate and learn which foods and beverages were safe for our American stomachs. No Montezuma's Revenge for us, thank you.

My three fellow travelers, Adrienne, Jo Ann and Beryl Marie, were immediately renamed by Manuel

in his native Spanish to Adriana, Joanna and Mariá.
As Miki, I kept my name but gained the Mexican
pronunciation of "Meekee."

The four of us had joined together primarily because we all had wanted to follow the migration of
the Monarch butterflies. In addition, there was a
special interest in learning to speak more Spanish
and seeing the ancient ruins of Teotihuacán.

Of the group, only Adriana had been traveling to
various parts of Mexico for many years. Cuernavaca
holds a special place in her heart because her son-in-
law, Rafael, who now lives in Minnesota, had been
born there and still has many friends and relatives
here. With her connections, Adriana had been more
than happy to arrange for our guide and living accommodations. On both scores, we received so
much more than we had ever expected.

We were all extremely exhausted by early evening, but suddenly revived when the gates opened to
our very own villa, complete with a cook and a
maid. I define our lodgings as a villa because it more
than met the dictionary definition of a large and

luxurious home rented for a vacation, a suburban residence of a wealthy person. It had, in fact, once been open on a tour of exceptional homes in Cuernavaca. Each of us had her own bedroom with bath, plus a hot tub and pool for all of us to enjoy after a long day of touring. Our travel budgets were not unlimited and we were all grateful to know that all this had been provided at an extremely reasonable rate, thanks to Adriana and her connections.

Once inside, we handed our groceries over to Consuela and Magdalena, who, for ease of pronunciation, we immediately renamed "Connie" and "Maggie." They giggled at their new names and promptly pampered us with snacks and margaritas. What a life!

After allowing us to relax and enjoy our surroundings for a bit, Manuel summarized our plans for the next day. We would be seeing the sights of Cuernavaca and learning some of Mexico's important legends. He told us that each day, he would be giving us an *ofrenda*, translated as an offering or special gift. This gift of understanding or awareness would be delivered to us as we were relaxing or driving from destination to destination. That first night, he left us with the words: "Today your *ofrenda* is ADVENTURE. By intelligently assessing the perceived dangers involved and then going ahead and making this trip, you have given this gift to yourselves and you need to acknowledge this.

"Travel is the highest form of adventure. When you travel, you become child-like, curious, innocent and intuitive. You leave your everyday life behind and discover more of your true self through the experience of how those in other cultures live. You essentially break free of your comfort zone. Learning another language, even if only a few words and phrases, helps you become more at one with the people you are visiting. Record and remember this adventure through your videos, photos, souvenirs and journals, because among yourselves, you will be able to relive these times, but even with all this, your families and friends will never have quite the same appreciation that you do for what you have experienced. The old saying still holds true, you really had to be there.

"Get ready to relax, and experience, because tomorrow, and for the remainder of your trip, you will be on my time — 'Mexican time,' Manuel continued. "No more tight schedules and calendars. No carpools, computers, and cell phones. Only the slow, continuous, circular motion of the hands of the clock. Rest up, be ready and I will be here sometime before noon. As they say in your country, we will go with the flow."

Cuernavaca

It was the gun that woke us the next morning. Actually, it was Joanna's discovery of the gun lying on the shelf in her closet. She was the best of us to find it, because her husband is a retired law enforcement officer and she was comfortable with having a gun around the house. The rest of us, however, were not. Magdalena, our maid, explained that the handgun was for the protection of our wealthy hosts and their guests, but for us it became yet another reminder that we must always be alert to danger.

The day began with a light breakfast and the return of Manuel who would introduce us to the colorful history and myth to be discovered in Cuernavaca, a playground for the rich and famous, both Mexican and American. How fitting that we travelers, as we entered the fortress-like Catedral de la Asunción, should first be greeted by a more than life size statue of St. Christopher, the patron saint of travelers. Manuel commented that St. Christopher is his favorite saint and he further explained that he started our tour with the cathedral because the church is where life is centered in each Mexican community. As a Catholic himself, he pointed out that more than ninety percent of the population of Mexico is Roman Catholic and that we would be visiting a lot of churches. None of our group was Catholic, so we all had a lot to learn about the symbolism of his religion.

As we started to truly understand the concept that things are never quite as they appear, we found that the Catholic Church in Mexico is literally built on duality. This Cathedral was most likely constructed on the ruins of an Aztec temple using those very same stones from the ruins of that temple to build the church. Sacred Indian idols were sometimes secretly buried beneath the newer Catholic statues and were known only to the Indians themselves so that when they were required to worship Christ, they were actually continuing to worship their own gods at the same time.

After thoroughly exploring the cavernous Cathedral from top to bottom, and learning all about religious architectural elements from our very own architect, we decided that it was time to experience some authentic tortilla soup and enchiladas. Manuel mentioned as we were leaving the church that if this had been Sunday, we could have attended the legendary and lively Mariachi Mass accompanied by spirited guitars, trumpets and violins. As we exited into the courtyard, we were suddenly accosted by a large group of beggars of all ages from young street urchins to feeble old ones with outstretched skeletal arms, some holding infants. This was a jolting reminder that so many in the world do not even begin to enjoy the same advantages we have in our everyday life in America.

Once we gave out some pesos to those in need, Joanna, who had been busy videotaping the church, grabbed our attention. She asked if we had noticed the small shadowy figure hiding off to the side who seemed to have been so intently watching our every move. None of us, including Manuel, had noticed anything unusual. After scolding Joanna for reading too many mystery novels, we continued on to our first Mexican restaurant meal. We were each well prepared by taking our daily protective dose of Pepto Bismol, just in case we somehow slipped up and ate or drank something we shouldn't. The meal was just as wonderful as we had anticipated and we were glad that we had contributed to those at the church so that they also would have a proper meal.

Manuel explained over lunch that our *ofrenda* for the day was MYTH and that as a Mexican Indian of Aztec origins who speaks the Aztec language, Nahuatl, he has been honored to help pass down their myths, legends, traditions and customs from person to person and generation to generation. "This gift of myth both perpetuates the past and enriches the future. It is the magic of myth that has enabled the Aztec culture to somehow survive its brutal destruction. Each of you, by the way, will undoubtedly create your own myth sometime during our adventures."

Next door to the Church was Cuernavaca's most visited sight, *Jardín Borda* (Borda Gardens). Wealthy silver magnate José de la Borda built this vacation home in the late 1700s. The beautiful gardens, actually a huge private park with a man-made lake, have, after many years of decay, been restored to their former glory. You can close your eyes and imagine those of wealth and royalty whiling away their hours here in the past. It was very soothing to the soul to sit quietly for a few minutes ourselves, while the calm lake waters reflected our thoughts of the wonderful things yet to come on our trip.

As we continued the tour of Cuernavaca, we would see the Palace of Hernán Cortés and learn the famous myth of Quetzalcóatl and the stories of Cortés, Montezuma, and the overthrow of Mexico by the Spanish. Cuernavaca is the capital of the state of Morelos, and as such housed the Cortés Palace which later became the state legislative headquarters. Now a museum, they proudly display accordion folded amate paper codices that recorded the important day-to-day history of the Aztecs with words composed of colorful pictures. Most of these codices were destroyed by the Spanish during and after the conquest, so it was very thrilling to actually see some of the few that survived.

For us, the most impressive part of the museum was the massive Diego Rivera mural covering the entire wall of the east portico. The famous mural, commissioned by former Ambassador Dwight Morrow, father of Anne Morrow Lindbergh, depicts the history of Cuernavaca with vast emotion. Manuel showed us that by using vivid colors and graphic, larger-than-life scenes, this painting portrays how the diverse people of Mexico, whether Aztec or Spanish, have initiated or experienced bloodshed by sacrifice, conquest, inquisition or revolution. He pointed out that his countrymen and actually all of us are more alike in our transgressions against our fellow man than we would like to believe or admit.

Mexico as we know it today really began with the ancient myth of Quetzalcóatl, the "Feathered Serpent." Half quetzal bird, half serpent, he was a gentle god, the god of the wind, who commanded his followers to be loving and peaceful. Unlike his dark skinned people, he was tall, light skinned and bearded. He asked simply for gifts of butterflies in a culture which required an unrelenting supply of blood from live human hearts. Wars were constantly waged by the war god Tezcatlipoca especially to capture live prisoners to sacrifice to all the other bloodthirsty gods. Tezcatlipoca shamed Quetzalcóatl and drove him away because of his peaceful beliefs. This contest between gods shows the duality of good versus evil which existed in the religion of the region. As the myth ends, the shamed Quetzalcóatl sailed east across the sea on a raft made of serpents, vowing to return in the year one-reed to reclaim his lands and rule his kingdom.

According to the Aztec calendar, the year one-reed was 1519, which coincided with the end of a fifty-two year cycle and meant turbulent times and great change. How very true this would actually prove to be. The mighty Aztec empire had become prosperous and was thriving beyond all imagination. Tenochtitlán, the capital city, in the middle of Lake Texcoco, was the largest city it the world—larger than Rome, Paris or London. Now called Mexico City, it is still according to most counts, the largest city in the world and Lake Texcoco has long since been filled in and dried up to make the city even larger.

As the year 1519 arrived, the Aztec king, Montezuma, was already experiencing unexplainable phenomena such as sudden floods, streaking comets and spontaneous fires. When his runners from the gulf coast reported strange vessels sailing towards them from the east, he was resigned to the fact that this was the predicted return of Quetzalcóatl. The fact was further confirmed in his mind when the men landed and their leader emerged, coincidentally, as a tall white man with a beard.

The man was in reality the Spanish conqueror, Hernán Cortés, and he couldn't have had a luckier reception. Montezuma welcomed him with open arms as the returning god of the Aztecs and showered him with gifts of gold, jewels, food, drink, and hospitality. When Montezuma ultimately discovered that Cortés was not a god but merely a man intent on capturing his gold, his people and his lands, it was much too late. The conquest had begun in earnest and Montezuma's simple military culture of bows, arrows and clubs could not withstand the more sophisticated guns, horses and metal armor of the Spanish soldiers.

After Cortés landed, he burned his ships to insure that his men would be sufficiently motivated not to flee. Because many towns in the Aztec empire were unhappy at paying tribute to Montezuma, Cortés was able to encourage the armies from these towns surrounding Tenochtitlén to join him in his fight. Cortés and his men also had an unintended weapon which helped to easily conquer the Aztecs and that was smallpox. There was no built-up immunity among the Indians and so a great many of them died without ever seeing battle. When the conquest was complete, life in Mexico would never be the same.

When we returned to our villa for the evening, we were greeted by our cook, Consuela, and the inviting aroma of a marvelous dinner of chicken mole and Mexican rice. Our simple groceries, with the addition of Consuela's own ingredients including chocolate, chiles and special spices, had been transformed into this national treasure. Adriana had even invited guests for *la comida*, a middle-aged couple from Minnesota who were attending one of the Spanish immersion language schools for which Cuernavaca is so well known. This was a great introduction to living the language for Mariá, who being the most adventurous of us all, would be staying on for two additional weeks after the rest of us left, to live with a Mexican family, attending a language school, and speaking only Spanish.

The guest couple proved to be the entertainment

for the evening. While traveling together, they found they really didn't like each other very much, on this extremely long date, and couldn't wait to finish up their travel commitment to each other and part ways. Much to our amusement, the subtle and not so subtle sparks really flew both in English and Spanish. As we all ended the evening, Manuel reminded us to rest well because tomorrow we would hit the road for a few days on our journey to find the butterflies. We would begin with an overnight stay in the colonial city of Morelia. Because we would be heading deep into the mountains, Manuel asked that we leave any valuables and most of our cash in our safe at the villa. He also asked us to dress down and look as little like affluent Americans as possible, just to play it safe.

Morelia

Manuel appeared on his white horse at eight forty-three, the white horse being his vintage white van which had seen many Mexican miles. This was definitely no luxury limousine, but it generally got the job done. Manuel had obviously spent some extra time polishing and vacuuming his trusty steed for our benefit. We didn't get very far into the mountains before exhaust fumes became an uncomfortable problem to those of us seated on the middle and back seats. Manuel found a mechanic in the next small town to take a look.

The whole episode reminded us of *Sanford & Son* or some similar television sit-com. The run-down shop contained so many ancient auto parts that they probably could have assembled a complete vintage vehicle from parts alone. The mechanic quickly and proficiently welded an extension on our broken tail-pipe using an open flame within inches of the gas tank. All we could picture was the whole thing blowing up, along with our entire trip, but about an hour and only $6 later we were on the road again --- fume-free.

We had come from Minnesota just days before, where everything lacked color, including the frozen snow covered landscape and the pale skinned, win-ter weary people. The most amazing thing about the day was all the vibrant color we encountered every-where, in the abundant and unusual flowers and trees, the thick green grass, the richly dark-skinned people and their colorful clothes, crafts, food, music and language. Even if the temperature wasn't as hot as it actually was, it would still have seemed so with all of those warm colors surrounding us.

This would prove to be a very long and arduous day of traveling through winding, scary mountain roads, but a full day well spent reaching Morelia. The butterflies were a day and a half from Cuernavaca by way of Morelia, and getting the longest part of the trip behind us today would allow us plenty of time to spend in the charming town of Pátzcuaro tomorrow. Those hours confined in the van gave Manuel more than a chance to delve deeply into his *ofrenda* for the day: DIVERSITY.

In his best professorial manner, Manuel taught us that "the Mexican people are a very successful blending of Spanish and Indian blood and cultures, just as the mole sauce we had for dinner the night before was a fine blending of unlikely and unrelated ingredients. Humans of all races are more alike than different. Science has shown that we are all ninety-nine percent the same no matter what we look like or where we come from, and we all share the same basic desires to be able to take care of our families, enjoy our friends and have a good life. Because we are so much alike, life could become much more satisfying and much more colorful if we would only learn to truly cherish our differences. Our differences are what spice up our lives."

Manuel continued: "Red, the color of blood, is the one color that everyone in the universe shares in common, but it takes all colors for God to make a rainbow. All cultures have special things to teach one another and they each have a unique purpose in life, as do individuals. The Aztec priests prophesied that this would be the age in which all the peoples of the world would mingle their blood. We, as humans, are all in this together and we only have one world to share among us. This new millennium will eventually provide the pieces to the puzzle so that we can all willingly evolve together toward world peace and prosperity."

Once we reached Morelia, the capitol of the state of Michoacán, our task was to find a hotel for the night. We were in luck right away with rooms for all of us at Hotel Casino, a trusted guidebook recommendation. Their sidewalk restaurant, considered the best in town, was just what we needed, and we all enjoyed their renowned whitefish dinner. Manuel excused himself for a few minutes and when he returned he explained that he had "bought some Mexican insurance," meaning he had taken the distributor cap off of his engine so that the van was immobilized for anyone wishing to take it for an uninvited ride.

Now we were desperate for a walk after riding all day and such a filling meal, so Manuel happily took us to the Cathedral for our church of the day. While walking we were constantly wandering in and out of courtyards and found one that was particularly intriguing. We learned that it was attached to a former monastery now utilized as a college. One of the students offered us an impromptu tour and Manuel, as an architect, was especially fascinated to find how creatively the monks' quarters had been put to use. Each sparse, stone-walled, cell-like room was now a student's dorm room, complete with the requisite television, stereo and computer. We all, however, were very grateful to be returning to our own more modern and spacious rooms at the hotel to turn in for the night.

Morelia, which didn't even bring out Joanna's video camera, ultimately proved to be the least interesting place that we visited, probably because we had little time to spend there and because we had bigger whitefish to fry, so to speak.

On to Pátzcuaro!

Pátzcuaro

After an early start and A morning's ride from Morelia, suddenly right in front of us was the sparkling jewel of Lake Pátzcuaro. And there were the fishermen with their famous butterfly shaped nets. This was the source of last night's dinner of translucent whitefish, the only source of *pescado blanco* in the world. This lake is also the only source of a tiny smelt-like fish, fried whole and served as a snack with lemon and chiles. For now we needed to pass right on by to find hotel rooms for the night.

Mision San Manuel offered a very fitting name

and splendid balconies overlooking the plaza. Once again we were in luck and found all the rooms we needed. When we were situated, being true red-blooded all-American shoppers, we rushed to the many shops surrounding the plaza to purchase some of the legendary local crafts. Adriana had told me about the Cross of Miracles made in that region, and that was what I was seeking. These crosses are covered with *milagros*, small metal charms that are tacked down on the surface, representing every facet of life, and by focusing on a specific charm you are supposed to be provided whatever miracle you request. I'm not sure it really works, but just in case, why not? I found the one cross that seemed to speak to me and then we moved on to look at paper flowers, hand painted pottery, rugs, baskets, embroidery, metalwork, cutwork and wood carvings. While Adriana was busy bargaining, Joanna was busy videotaping, and we were all busy shopping.

Satisfied with our souvenirs, it was time to return to the lakeshore to catch the launch to Janitzio, a big bulge of an island in the middle of Lake

Pátzcuaro. The launch runs all day long whenever the seats are filled, which is approximately every thirty minutes, and is a marvelous mix of tourists and natives. While wandering the shops earlier, we had purchased Mexican cheese, buns and sweet pastries for our lunch aboard the launch, so we fit right in with the natives enjoying their own picnic lunches. The island features a giant statue of Mexico's beloved military hero José Morelos at the very top and offers a workout for the day to those who climb the steep stone steps to pay their respects. Adriana, Joanna, Mariá and Manuel made the climb, but I decided to save myself for the climb to the butterflies the next day. While the others were off on their adventure, I busied myself with trying out my newfound Spanish on anyone who was willing to listen.

When we returned to Pátzcuaro we discovered that the plaza was teeming with activity. Preparations were being made for a festival that is held only once every hundred years. The Basílica de Nuestra Señora de la Salud houses the Virgin of Health perched on the main altar. The beautiful virgin was fashioned of solid corn stalk pulp and mucilage because the Catholic priests were afraid if she were made of cloth, the Indians could hide their own idol underneath. She is very beloved, supposedly vested with special healing powers and is ceremoniously paraded through Pátzcuaro at the beginning of each century. That would be happening tonight, and it obviously would only happen once in a lifetime for us and for most of the other spectators.

As we strolled the plaza, we discovered a most amazing thing. A portion of the sidewalk was blocked off all the way around the plaza and covered in sawdust. Indians were taking hand-made templates and colored sawdust and decorating sections with their own unique multi-colored patterns and designs. It was all very unusual, but most importantly quite spectacular. We also discovered that the plaza would be the scene of the festival parade that evening, and as it so happened, we had ring side seats on our balconies. We were able to get these rooms so easily because the locals came only for the evening and did not spend the night. Manuel told us that in addition, tonight would be the first lunar eclipse of the new millennium. A total lunar eclipse happens only rarely when the earth's shadow passes over the full moon. Because an eclipse of the moon is easily visible to the naked eye, all people on the same half of the earth can easily experience this phenomenon at the same time. The likelihood of the centennial celebration of the *Virgin de la Salud* and a total eclipse of the moon ever happening on the same night was almost non-existent. We felt truly fortunate to have unknowingly stumbled onto all of these rare events.

It didn't seem necessary to have dinner because all of us had been grazing on local foods all day long, so we opted to just settle in for drinks and snacks on one of our balconies. Darkness descended while we were waiting for the festival to begin below, and Manuel spent this time relating our *ofrenda* for the day: RITUAL. "Tonight you will experience just one of the thousands of festivals or fiestas that are celebrated each year in my country. The practice of ritual or tradition celebrated as religious or secular events is what cements cultures and communities. When our government tourist office attempted to catalog all the annual public fiestas in our country, it took more than two hundred pages. On any day you can find a fiesta somewhere in Mexico and each and every one is unique.

"Ritual is what gives custom, familiarity and structure to our everyday life. It gives us something to look forward to. It enriches what in our culture can otherwise be very hard and difficult lives. Every culture has its own rituals including baptism, confirmation and marriage, and families need to honor these and create their own, starting with birthdays, anniversaries and other special family occasions. Something as simple as eating dinner together can become a family ritual. Now we are going to experience a large scale religious ritual in the plaza below."

As darkness descended, the procession began. Hundreds of Catholic priests, led by the Cardinal from Mexico City, were preceded by the *Virgin de la Salud* across the sawdust decorated sidewalk. The virgin and the mile of marching priests were honored as if they were royalty, and as she passed along, golden fireworks were set off in the trees above the crowd. Sparks showered down on the heads of the unconcerned onlookers. This would never have been allowed to happen in our strictly safety conscious society.

With the crowd following behind, the *Virgin de la Salud* was then reverently paraded up the hill for two steep blocks to the basilica, to once again be installed on her pedestal for the next hundred years. We left our balcony and followed along and when she was secure on the altar, there was a magnificent burst of multi-colored fireworks to rival any we had ever seen. An older Mexican man, who was caught up in the fast paced music, grabbed Mariá and quickly danced her feet off. Meanwhile, as we looked overhead, the moon became totally eclipsed, as if nature itself was acknowledging the Virgin by completely darkening the sky for her fireworks display. We felt specially blessed to have witnessed all we did that evening—a fitting prelude to the spectacle of the butterflies the next day.

Angangueo

The butterflies beckoned and we were ready. We had been anticipating this day for more than a year and we got off to our earliest start yet, six-thirty in the morning. Manuel was equally as excited as we were because he, like us, had never seen the marvelous Monarchs in their winter home. The Mariposa Monarca Butterfly Sanctuary, consisting of five separate areas, is nestled in the eastern region of Michoacán. El Rosario and Sierra Chincua are the only two open to the public. El Rosario was the original and is the easiest to access but consequently the most crowded. We were heading on to

Sierra Chincua. Visitors to either sanctuary must enter from Ocampo or Angangueo.

As we drove, Manuel explained that Monarch butterflies start their yearly cycle in the spring as a tiny fertilized egg laid on the underside of a leaf of a milkweed plant somewhere in the southern part of the United States. The resulting butterfly continues north, mating and laying more eggs on milkweed plants and then dies. This cycle continues throughout the summer for three or four generations reaching as far north as Canada. The final generation lives the longest and before winter sets in has the difficult job of migrating all the way to Mexico, surviving over the winter and mating to once again start north in the spring, when it lays the first generation of eggs in the southern United States and then dies. During the migration, the amazing Monarch butterfly travels through the United States, from Mexico to Canada, connecting cultures and continents.

We passed through Ocampo and arrived at the town of Angangueo in time for an early lunch, but none of us was hungry. We were too anxious so we simply snacked again. As we made our way through town, we were approached by many men and boys offering to be our paid guide. We didn't need a guide to the Sanctuary or transportation so we kept waving them on. Soon there were so many of them that we were forced to completely ignore them. The van kept climbing through cobblestone streets that were so narrow we could almost touch the buildings on either side through the windows of our van. Once we reached the sign for the entrance, we found there was actually no road at all, but a very well worn, rocky, rutted path through a field into the forest. We carefully advanced the van through the trees until we came to the base of the mountain.

Here is where we paid our fee and were introduced to our guide. Now we could only continue on foot or on horseback. Having been on horseback but twice in my life, I was not really crazy about riding a horse two miles up a mountain, yet climbing on foot seemed even worse. Joanna was not any happier, because in her youth she had a very bad experience on horseback. She felt the best horses were those on a carousel. Mariá was thrilled with the idea because she owns horses and rides all the time, and Adriana is always game for anything that isn't life threatening. Manuel made all of the arrangements for us. We picked out our horses, and were each lead up the mountain by an Indian on foot, kind of like a child being lead around a pony ring.

The ride actually proved to be fun for all of us. When we reached a large clearing at the top, we left the horses and were then lead an additional mile on foot down the other side of the mountain. The horses were left behind because they create so much noise and dust that it is disturbing to the butterflies. Walking down the mountainside was easy enough but we kept wondering when we would see the butterflies. We were carried along by our curiosity. First there were only one or two circling above our heads, no different than we had seen at home. As we walked further, more began to gather, until there were many groups of a dozen or more following us.

Then suddenly, there they were, millions of

Monarchs. The sight was so much more than any of us had ever imagined. To say it was breathtaking would be an understatement, beyond the scope of mere words. The quiet sound of millions of fluttering wings was surely God whispering to us. As we approached, we were asked to remain silent and keep still in respect to our soaring friends. The native Oyamel fir trees are home to the migrating Monarchs with thousands clinging to each tree. Our lasting visual impression was of a forest in the fall with trees covered in colorful leaves, but here the "leaves," instead of falling, when they are warmed enough by the sun, they fluttered gracefully to the sky, forming an incredible golden-orange cloud.

We were left alone the whole time and were allowed to sit silently on fallen logs for over an hour in this natural cathedral. We learned later that Manuel had told our guide that we were worthy and respectful women and so he had taken us to a very special and secluded area, one where he doesn't take loud tourists and school groups because they tend to easily forget to be silent and still. The butterflies playfully landed on our hair and clothing and by landing on our cheeks and fluttering their fabulous wings, they covered each of us with many sweet butterfly kisses. We wanted to stay forever, but eventually it was time to move on.

What went down, must go back up, and so, unfortunately, we had to climb back up for a mile to meet the horses. The high altitude made it very difficult to breathe, and not being in the best of shape, we took it very, very slowly, stopping often to literally gasp in the thin mountain air. Manuel was quite fit and used to the high altitude, so he moved right along with ease and continued to cheer us on. We all agreed that as difficult as this was, it had been well worth the effort to see the butterflies---an experience we would never forget. When we finally spied the horses at the top, we all suddenly became instant horse lovers.

The base of the mountain was now bustling with tourists and souvenir and food vendors. We took our time picking out t-shirts and postcards that would always remind us of this very special day, plus show everyone back home that we four unlikely grandmothers had really climbed the mountain and visited the butterflies. Because the impoverished Indians are now able to earn a living escorting the tourists and selling souvenirs and food, they in turn take great care to preserve their inviting natural habitat and their valuable resource, the migrating Monarchs.

We loaded our tired bodies into the van and headed back down the rocky rutted path to Angangueo. The plan was to drive back to Cuernavaca that evening. Manuel took this opportunity to relate our *ofrenda* for the day: THE STRUGGLE. "The Struggle is defined by the life cycle or four stages of growth of the Monarch butterfly. The first stage is the egg (infancy) which quickly hatches into a tiny caterpillar (childhood). The caterpillar constantly eats and sheds its skin several times until it has doubled its size many times over, eventually turning into a cocoon or chrysalis (adulthood). This hardened case protects the developing butterfly. The metamorphosis is complete with the fourth stage, when the delicate butterfly breaks free from the hardened cocoon and soars into the world (wise elderhood). It has always been fascinating to me to know that the word chrysalis originates from the Greek word for gold, possibly because the chrysalis of the Monarch butterfly is actually sparsely studded with what looks like fourteen-karat gold.

"It is a very difficult job for the butterfly to break out of the cocoon, but if any help is given, it will die. The butterfly needs the struggle to fully develop. Humans also need struggle in their lives in order to grow. A life without struggle is like a muscle that is not exercised. The struggle is what makes us strong. Without the struggle we are not growing and learning and are simply counting time until we die. Like the butterfly, as wise elders, we each need to break free to finally test our wings." Mariá commented that she had often felt strong yet fragile at the same time, just like a Monarch butterfly.

As we were traveling on the main highway toward Toluca, we started up yet another steep incline, when suddenly smoke started pouring out from under the hood. We just barely made it to the top and had to stop. We pulled to the side to wait and see if the engine was simply overheated. This of course was just when we all needed to use the bathroom, so in our best Minnesota backwoods manner, we took turns disappearing into the woods at the side of the road. With high spirits we looked on our situation as just another part of the great adventure, but being broken down at the side of the highway in Mexico, when darkness would soon be approaching is not where Manuel wanted us to be. To him, we were like sitting ducks. It was about now that he started wishing we had brought along that gun from the safe at the villa.

When Manuel tried to start the engine again, it wouldn't start. We had stopped just over the crest of the mountain, so he loaded us in and we coasted down to the small town of Santa Mariá at the bottom. As luck would have it, there was a mechanic, another *Sanford & Son*, on our side of the highway, so we coasted right on in. Manuel instructed us not to speak while we were sitting there—the second time that day we were required to remain silent. Our speaking would alert the mechanics that we were Americans and since we were totally at their mercy, we could easily be taken advantage of. The problem was diagnosed as a bad alternator and we would have to leave the van there until morning to have it repaired. At least the van had gotten us through the most important part of our day.

Because this was a very small town, there were no overnight accommodations. That was a major problem until, as if right on cue, the bus to Mexico City appeared on the horizon. Manuel flagged it down for us. We left the van for repair and all of us with our various belongings piled onto the bus. What a relief, but we were not surprised at all that Manuel could make magic happen. After several hours we arrived at one of the bus terminals in Mexico City, took a taxi across town to another terminal for a bus to Cuernavaca and then took a taxi home. It was well after midnight and our villa would never look more inviting. Consuela and Magdalena had been very worried about us and were there to greet us with warm smiles and welcoming arms. Our guard dog Greta, a friendly, but most effective, large black lab was also happy to see us.

Manuel called his wife to pick him up at the villa, and then told us that tomorrow, once he retrieved the repaired van, we would regroup in the evening to plan the remainder of our trip. His parting message to us was that we had "passed the test" and he would explain just how when we were together again. For now, he had gotten us safely home and that was all that really mattered.

Cuernavaca

We loved sleeping late. To me, the act of awakening to an alarm and getting up early every morning is like going through the trauma of being born over and over again. Sleeping late and waking naturally seems so much more humane. After three satisfying but stressful days on the road, how wonderful that we would be able to spend a whole carefree day relaxing at home.

Because it was Sunday and not a workday, Adriana immediately put out the word to family, extended family and friends that we would be at home, welcoming visitors all day long. This ultimately turned into one large ongoing family reunion. Rafael, Adriana's son-in-law, has nine brothers and sisters, plus their various spouses, children and grandchildren. His father had passed away, but his mother was our first guest, stopping by on her way home from mass. Since none of these people spoke much English, we had a lot of opportunity to practice our Spanish all day long.

Consuela had fed us a late breakfast of *huevos rancheros*, after which we took on the job of doing our laundry. At our request, Magdalena showed us where to find the washer and dryer, but she couldn't believe that we would possibly want to do this chore ourselves. She felt that was her job. It puzzled her even more when we chose not to use the dryer and opted instead to hang our clothes from a line we installed in the trees in the courtyard to get the glorious benefit of having them dry in the sun and fresh air. This was all too familiar to her, too much like the many primitive yards full of clothes hanging to dry that we had passed in the mountains just yesterday. Having modern technology at her fingertips, she now much preferred using the dryer.

We met Paco, the pool and yard boy, a small Aztec looking and seemingly street-wise young man, when he was called upon to start up the hot tub for us. He told us he was attempting to learn English and would really appreciate practicing by speaking with and listening to us. As we lounged in the sun we commented on how wondrous it was that we had ever connected to make this trip. We were all from the community of Wayzata, Minnesota, a suburb of Minneapolis located on the northern shore of Lake Minnetonka; we had crossed paths from time to time during the past twenty-five years, through school, church and civic activities, but we were still simply passing acquaintances.

We remembered how fate had brought us together that day at our local coffee shop where we somehow discovered that we were all wanting to go to Mexico to see the butterflies. We marveled at how four mere acquaintances could actually pull this trip together, and turn out to be so completely compatible, just like lifelong friends. We were very diverse women, yet we discovered we all had a large social conscience and a passion for travel in common. It helped that we had experienced many of the same things in our community throughout the years. Even if we weren't friends at the time, essentially we shared a lot of the same history.

As we soaked up the sun, we pondered the fact that the gift of The Struggle was very familiar to each of us. Between all of us we had faced within our families many of the major struggles of life—death and divorce, unemployment and financial loss, depression and mental illness, alcoholism and eating disorders, serious illness and life threatening accidents. Yes, Manuel was right; The Struggle had made us strong, and now we cherished with gratitude all the many good things in our lives.

Just as we were getting a little too serious, Adriana's funny friends, Marta and Carmen, popped in to say hello and offer their own Mexican version of an American Tupperware type party. They are sisters but are as different as night and day, both in appearance and personality. Marta is fair-haired, quiet and serious and Carmen is brunette, boisterous and bigger than life. Together they are very, very funny. Their product was silver jewelry, handcrafted by a very talented friend. I bought a handsome ring with a stone that looked somewhat similar to a garnet, my birthstone. Knowing what a great bargain all of this was, Adriana bought dozens of pairs of silver earrings to sell in a little shop back home.

Carmen's son Omar stopped in just long enough to retrieve Carmen and Marta and drive them to their next appointment. He would return on another day to visit. The relatives streamed through all afternoon. Besides Mamá Enedina, there were sisters Cecilia, Mercedes, Olivia and Luz Elena, plus brothers Julio, Pedro, Federico, Carlos and Alberto. Also in attendance was an assortment of aunts, uncles, nieces, nephews, wives, husbands, children and grandchildren, not to mention a few other unrelated friends of the family. Adriana had met all these people through the years at family gatherings and they were very happy to see her and meet her American friends.

The extended family is the center of daily life in Mexico, with everyone making his or her special contribution. Several generations often live together or at least close to one another, in houses or apartments in the city or on small plots of land in the countryside. Grandparents, parents, aunts, uncles and children always celebrate together even if they don't live together. Children are taught to honor their parents and grandparents. Older people are respected and tell family stories and give welcomed advice. Grown-up sons and daughters feel a responsibility to take care of their aging family members. In Mexico, family absolutely comes first.

After all the day's activity, we were glad to eat dinner alone. At our request, Consuela had gone to the market and purchased four small red snappers. We had asked her to make *huachinanga a la veracruzana*, a fish dish consisting of red snapper fillets baked in a sauce of tomatoes, pimento stuffed green olives, sliced onions and green chiles. Consuela worked hard on the meal, but we had fillets in mind, not the whole fish, staring up with beady eyes, that she served to each of us. In addition, the fish were still practically raw. We guessed that our normally excellent cook did not understand this dish. We did not want to insult Consuela after her great effort, so we picked at and pushed the fish around on our plates and ate all of the surrounding rice and beans. The next day was to be her day off, so we volunteered that we would clean up the dinner dishes and sent her on home for the evening, so that we could diplomatically salvage the "leftover" fish for us to cook properly and save for fish tacos on another night.

Manuel arrived after dinner. He was glad to see that we had such a fun and refreshing day, and was very pleased to have been able to spend some time with his own family. After they attended mass, his wife had driven him back to Santa Mariá to pick up the van which he reported was repaired at a reasonable price and was working just fine. We sat on the patio to do our planning, surrounded by giant poinsettias the size of table tops. We were impressed to learn that the poinsettia had originated in Cuernavaca.

Manuel gave us FAMILY as our *ofrenda* for the day, commenting that "it has been a wonderful family day for all of us. You have had a chance to meet most of Adriana's family members and friends here in Cuernavaca. I can tell that you are all quite family oriented from the way you talk about your own children and grandchildren. It was very surprising for me to find out that you have not all been lifelong friends. From what I can see, the four of you are very like-minded and have in just a few days had a chance to bond as your own 'family of friends.' Good friends are like relatives that you get to choose for yourself.

"Last night I told you that you had passed the test. The test was my needing to know that each of you possess a special spirit of camaraderie plus many talents and gifts that influence others in a positive way. We were broken down on the side of the road in a situation which could have been very dangerous, but there was no complaining or whining. You just silently prayed for a solution, had faith in me to get the job done, and then graciously accepted each moment for what it was worth.

"My ancestors, through my Aztec priest, have instructed me to assist him in divulging an ancient Aztec message to those I am with during the first eclipse of the moon at the beginning of the new millennium. That is, of course, if they prove worthy of this wisdom. You are those people, and you have proven yourselves quite worthy. We will all learn this message together on the last day of our tour, when we go to the ruins of Teotithuacán. The Palace of the Butterfly God at Teotihuacán sits in the shadow of the Pyramid of the Moon and is where the message will be given. In just a few more days, from out of that shadow will come ancient knowledge."

We were spellbound. Manuel had certainly passed our test as a perfect guide and a fine human being, and we were anxious to learn his message. Just as we were finishing making our plans, Paco announced to Manuel in Spanish that he was shutting down the hot tub for the evening and would return the next afternoon to start it up again for us.

Once Paco left, Magdalena told Manuel that Paco seemed to be listening to our every word. He explained that Paco was only trying to listen to as much English as possible. For the remainder of our time, we would be doing day trips, beginning tomorrow with Miacatlán and a visit to the orphanage to take gifts to the children and for Adriana to meet face to face, for the first time, the student she had been sponsoring.

Miacatlán

Family absolutely comes first in Mexico. That is what we learned just yesterday. But what if you don't have a family? What if you are dropped off as an infant on the doorstep of an orphanage? What if both of your parents die and there is nobody to take care of you or your brothers and sisters? What if you are the accidental child of a prostitute or your father is in jail? These are the questions that Father Bill Wasson has answered for thousands of Mexican children, starting in 1954, with one abandoned boy who was living on the streets of Cuernavaca and was arrested for stealing money for food. Father Bill rescued him from going to jail and soon was asked to take in more and more children. That was the beginning of *Nuestros Pequeños Hermanos* in the small nearby village of Miacatlán.

Joanna, Mariá and I went to the orphanage that day feeling that this would be a rather sad and depressing experience. Adriana assured us that it would not. *Nuestros Pequeños Hermanos*, she announced, is a happy place filled with genuine love and caring. She guaranteed that we would come away with our spirits lifted to heights we could never imagine.

Manuel had given us some background information on the orphanage during our short drive there. Located in what was once a large hacienda, the more than nine thousand acres are surrounded by a high wall and a visitor must enter through massive bolted wooden doors. They are not bolted to keep the children in, because the children have no desire to run away, but rather to keep out any harmful intruders. At any one time there are approximately eight hundred children living there from the smallest infant all the way up to age twenty.

We were let in the front doors and drove into a large cobblestone plaza with children of all ages, holding hands, laughing and happily crossing in every direction. Our doorman led us to the administration offices where we inquired about Juan Carlos, Adriana's godchild. This was the fourth child that she and Jack had sponsored through the years and this was her fourth visit to the orphanage. While Juan Carlos was being summoned, we went back to the plaza to get our gifts from the van. We had each brought an extra duffle bag to leave there, stuffed with clothes outgrown by our grandchildren. We each had also purchased small trinkets, gum and candy at home to hand out to as many of the children as we could. Adriana had also brought some gifts for Juan Carlos, ones that he had specifically requested.

After greetings and introductions, Juan Carlos volunteered to give us all a tour. What an amazing place this was. We saw his room, met his roommates and saw the rest of the complex, including the dining and recreational areas. Once the children reach a certain age, they are given age appropriate responsibilities. Everyone has a job that contributes to the good of the whole. These children have happily created their own family and become so bonded to all their brothers and sisters that they don't want to leave home any more than a child raised in a traditional Mexican family would want to leave his or her loving home. For this reason these children are always kept together with their siblings and are never allowed to be adopted by anyone outside of their own family. This is their home.

The jobs range from taking care of the smaller children, to raising crops, sweeping, cleaning, cooking and making by hand the three thousand tortillas a day that it takes to feed everyone. Most of the food that is eaten by the children and staff is grown and produced right there on the grounds. Life is not all work. There is, of course, church, school in the town of Miacatlán, and just plain having fun, with plenty of room to roam and an Olympic size swimming pool, given years ago by an anonymous donor who specified that the sizeable funds could only be used for a swimming pool and nothing else.

If students excel in their studies, they are even sent to college if they wish. Juan Carlos, who is now in high school, told us that he will eventually be going to law school. We were able to spend a little time among the adorable pre-schoolers with their big brown eyes that totally melted our hearts. Manuel was equally as captivated by the little ones as we were. Loving care abounds and sharing and service with a smile are the order of the day. When we said our goodbyes, Juan Carlos was beaming with pride to have had his own special visitors. Adriana was right, it is a happy place.

It was during the trip back to Cuernavaca that Manuel gave us our *ofrenda* for the day: LOVE. "God is often defined as pure love. When I speak of love, I am not talking about romantic love between men and women, but rather universal love or love for mankind as a whole. There are actually three kinds of love in the universe: love for ourselves, love for others, and love for mankind. There are also three ways in which we can express this love: physically, emotionally and intellectually. Today we have truly experienced the result of the deep love of mankind by those who so generously give their time, talent and treasure to those less fortunate than themselves. Plus we experienced the love that can develop among children for one another when a true feeling of family is established. At *Nuestros Pequeños Hermanos*, the children experience the blessings of both a very personal love and a universal love."

When Manuel dropped us off at the villa early in the afternoon, Paco was waiting to turn on the hot tub for us. While we waited for the water to warm, we decided to take a walk down the hill to a convenience store at the bottom to get some milk and eggs for our breakfast the next day. Magdalena warned us that we needed to be careful and watch our purses, to all stay together at all times, and to never take a walk outside our walls after dark. We saw why, when in broad daylight, we had to make our purchases through the bars on the door of the convenience store. You could not enter and go inside this small store, but instead had to ask for what you wanted and it was passed to you through the bars of the security gate which completely covered the front of the store. You paid for your purchase in the same manner, through the bars with small bills only. As we started our climb to the villa, there was Paco, on the corner, talking with a few friends. He gave us an embarrassed smile hello, like any young man might give his parents, and followed us back up the hill.

The water was just right by now, so we relaxed in the hot tub for a while before dressing for dinner at the famous *Las Mañanitas*. Consuela would not be there to cook for us, so we chose this as our big night out on the town. The taxi arrived and we were able to get a different view of Cuernavaca as we wove through the steep narrow streets. We passed the plaza and were amused by the colorful clowns and jugglers trying to earn a few pesos. The children seemed pleased with the large array of balloon animals that were for sale.

Las Mañanitas is considered by many to be one of the best restaurants in Mexico. They offer Mexican favorites with an international flair, though the food alone is not the only draw. The beautiful grounds with their parade of exotic birds captivated us. Peacocks, ostriches, flamingos and many other unusual birds roam freely among the diners on the terrace. Service and pampering are another specialty of the house. We had heard that this was a hangout for the rich and famous and were not surprised when our adorable waiter whispered to us that Harrison Ford and his party had been sitting at our table just the night before.

Over margaritas, we made our menu choices. Adriana decided on the fish, because she does not eat meat. Mariá ordered the Mexican Medley, which was actually a very upscale combination platter. Joanna played it as safe as you can get, ordering steak and fries, and we teased her that she could have that anywhere. I tried one of their signature dishes, a specially prepared flank steak surrounded by unusual potato flower petals. Being a food writer, everyone looked to me for my opinion, which was that the surroundings and service were spectacular, but that the food was really not all that special. To me, their reputation for excellent food had far outweighed the actual eating experience.

We had been having such a good time, laughing, joking and enjoying ourselves with such complete abandon, that a very handsome and prosperous looking Mexican gentleman at the next table sent over Kahlua after-dinner drinks for each of us with his compliments. We toasted him and our wonderful evening spent seeing how the affluent side of Mexico spends its time. We acknowledged that we each had a bit of Mother Teresa in us but we also agreed that having a bit of the good life doesn't hurt either. Today we had come face to face with the extremes of Mexican life. Another duality if you will—the wealth of the very successful versus the desperate poverty that could send a child to *Nuestros Pequeños Hermanos*. The best we could ask of ourselves was to appreciate and enjoy what we have, and always remember to help those who need our support. That is the highest kind of love we can offer. Tomorrow we would be traveling to the silver city of Taxco.

Taxco

Think of Mexico and you think of Aztec gold, the now mostly non-existent metal which made Mexico so worth conquering. But it was Mexican silver that endured and made Taxco the silver capital of the world. The town of Taxco, long ago declared a national monument, literally hangs from the mountainside, with streets so steep that taxis constantly travel up and down just to get the tourists around. The natives, however, are so used to the steep inclines that they gingerly move up and down on foot like mountain goats.

The trip to Taxco was highlighted by our *ofrenda* for the day, NATURE. It was nature, after all, that created both the beautiful gold and silver we value so much. We enjoyed noticing the unusual flowers, plants, trees, birds and animals that surrounded us in every direction. The bougainvillea abounds in shades of pinks, lavenders and oranges. The spectacular birds of paradise were probably the most familiar of the more unusual flowers. No wonder Mexican handcrafts are so colorful. The abundant colors of nature are simply incorporated into everything they create. In season, there are hundreds, if not thousands of acres of many shades of roses with frequent stands of rose merchants along the highway from Cuernavaca to Taxco. A bunch of two dozen roses would cost only about $3.00.

Manuel's studies have shown him that Mexico has one of the most complex, richest ecosystems on Earth. It has been estimated that more than fifty percent of all animal and plant species exist here because of the abundant precipitation and year round warmth. "All things in nature seem to survive because of an intricate system of symbiosis, and that includes us as humans as well. Symbiosis means to both give and receive at the same time. An easy example would be that when planting beans, the roots deposit nitrogen in the soil which is needed for the corn to grow. We in turn enjoy the riches of these naturally fertilized fields when we have our refried beans on corn tortillas. We then as humans must in turn remember to love and protect the earth. We always have to continue to be aware and caring of our natural resources in order for all of us to survive on this earth in peace."

Manuel told us about his most recent environmental endeavors and how he had won a coveted prize plus recognition at the University of Mexico for designing a unique and ecologically sound housing project. He went on further to explain how his ancestors made the best use of a sometimes uninviting natural environment in order to survive by creating *Chinampas*, or floating gardens. Farmlands were often scarce near the city. *Chinampas* were islands made around the marshy edges of a lake by piling up plants and nutrient rich mud, then holding this all together with wooden stakes. These man-made raised fields produced three crops a year and were tended and harvested by flat bottom canoe. Unfortunately, only a few of these fields still exist today.

As we carefully made our way to the silver market, we struggled with the severe steepness required to get there. Our recently repaired van did a good job for us though. Then as if with the wave of a magic wand there was more silver gathered together in the market than any of us had ever seen in one place at one time and at giveaway prices. There were more than two-hundred stalls with rows upon rows of handcrafted necklaces, bracelets, earrings, pins, charms, and everything imaginable. We all loaded up on gifts for family and friends and Manuel purchased some silver pieces and stones which he planned to assemble as necklaces for gifts. We even bought angel pins as a special thank-you for Consuela and Magdalena. It was certainly a good thing that Marta and Carmen had sold us their silver before our trip to Taxco.

While we searched for a place for lunch, we looked through the shops along the way for a silver St. Christophers's medal to give to Manuel to decorate his van. We figured he especially needed this to ward off any future mechanical problems. Adriana found the perfect one when we stumbled upon our church for the day, Santa Priesta y San Sebastián, situated on the Plaza Borda, easily one of the busiest town squares in all of Mexico. We had been hoping to see this breathtakingly beautiful landmark, given to Taxco by the wildly successful silver magnate, José de la Borda. It is said that a truly grateful de la Borda proclaimed, "God has given to de la Borda and now de la Borda gives to God." It is also said that he even offered to pave the road from Veracruz to Mexico City in silver coins if the Pope would only agree to a visit.

In this town so famous for silver, the church interior is ironically covered with ornamental gold on every possible decorative surface. Fortunately for future generations, this gold survived the Spanish conquest. We encountered and were invited to observe a beautiful wedding ceremony, uniting a Mexican bride and American groom, once again successfully continuing the melding of cultures. Finally our late lunch commenced three stories up inside a restaurant perched high atop the mountain. This made us feel we were truly on top of the world.

Because of so much rigorous climbing, we must have all dozed during our return trip, except for Manuel, of course. Before we knew it, we were back in Cuernavaca stopping to stock up on milk and eggs, snacks, beer and wine. Consuela had made fish tacos, guacamole and salsa for us. Manuel joined us for supper and a drink and taught us a traditional toast in Spanish: "*Arriba, abajo, al centro, por dentro!*," which translates roughly into: "drinks raised, drinks down, drinks clinking in the center, and finally down the hatch." Then, because Adriana had organized this trip for us, he asked her what specifically had brought her to see the butterflies. Adriana related the story of her brush with death.

On that fateful Thanksgiving day while Adriana

and Jack were walking, they had been talking about how she had just recently sold her quilting shop in Wayzata and that she now would have much more time to travel. A driver from a nearby house, in a hurry, had not adequately scraped the snow and ice from his car windows. The glare from the bright sun streaming through the windshield blinded the driver. Adriana was thrown fifty-two feet and landed on her head. Her right hand and knee were crushed and her face resembled raw hamburger embedded with gravel and dirt. The trauma physician said he couldn't believe she was still alive. She wasn't able to answer any simple questions such as her name or what day it was. She even thought that the current president was George Washington.

Having once been a nurse, Adriana was quite familiar with hospitals and doctors, however, she was shocked when she regained consciousness, not by the doctors and nurses surrounding her, but by the entire emergency room filled with at least four dozen spirits which explained themselves as angels sent to look over her. She was in excruciating pain, but couldn't be given any pain medication until they determined the extent of her injuries. It wasn't until four hours later that she was finally sedated and the surgeries on her hand, knee and face were performed simultaneously. It took over two hundred stitches in her face alone. Her broken ribs and fractured spine would have to heal on their own. Later the neurologist told her that the accident had severely traumatized her brain with a mind-numbing concussion, but that in the end her hard head was what had saved her. Jack agreed that the doctor certainly knew his Adriana!

Adriana told us that Mexico is what ultimately healed her. Jack is a golf pro and they spend every February in Mexico, away from winter, polishing his golf skills. She was determined to go that year, and against her doctor's protests, had promised to continue her physical therapy on the beach. It was just the medicine she needed. Her love for Mexico did the trick, and much to her doctor's amazement, helped her to progress at a rapid rate. Her hard head won out once again.

She continued to overcome memory loss and severe headaches, and to rehabilitate her leg and neck. The physical therapy lasted for five months, three hours a day for three times a week. The angels, incidentally, appeared by her bed each and every night until she was fully recovered. To see Adriana today, you would never know that any of this happened to her. Now Adriana once again had places to go and things she wanted to see. She had visited many parts of Mexico, such as Cuernavaca and Miacatlán, but everything else on the itinerary she created for us was also new to her. That day in Taxco, she purchased a very, very special silver pin for herself, a small grouping of angels.

Adriana loves to be in charge, and she is very good at it. When she ventured on this trip with us, she and Jack had just sold their large home of many years and purchased a much smaller fixer-upper house on a lovely little lake. Adriana was acting as the general contractor on the renovation of what would be their retirement home. She assigned Jack, with the help of their family and friends, the job of completely gutting the entire interior while she was in Mexico with us, including appliances, all décor and even several walls. This was well before the days of home makeovers on reality TV. Adriana's lesson was to let go, and let Jack do his job without her supervision. The accident had taught her that in the end she really couldn't control anything anyway, and now she was ready to test her new wings with us.

As Manuel left for the evening, he reminded us once again how perfect we were to receive the message at Teotihuacán. Paco, helpful as always, had the hot tub ready for us, after which we began a three evening card competition, a game called "May I", that Adriana taught us combining Poker and Rummy. From a cantina below our villa we could hear and enjoy the spirited strains of live Mexican music. We continued to practice our newly learned Mexican toast and reveled in the thought that tomorrow we would be exploring the well-known market at Tepoztlán.

Tepoztlán

Just like Sedona, Arizona or Machu Pichu, airplane needles can go crazy while flying over Tepoztlán. The valley of Tepoztlán and the surrounding mountains possess a healing magnetic force common to all other sacred spiritual sites of the world. It is believed by many that with the proper frame of mind of sincere intention and no expectations, it is possible to experience the cure of a physical or mental illness, simply by visiting any of the places in the world where this magical magnetic force is present.

This, however, was not the reason we came to Tepoztlán. The exceptional market was the true reason for our visit and the sacred qualities were just a welcome added bonus. The market at Tepoztlán is, in scope to Mexicans, what the Mall of America in Minnesota is to Americans. There were rows upon rows of outdoor stalls displaying pyramids of fruits and vegetables, slabs of meat, herbs, flowers, pottery and any other imaginable Indian handcrafts. Hernán Cortés once wrote that "in these markets they sell everything on earth...there is so much I can't remember it all and there is more I cannot name."

Mexico has given many familiar foods to the world of cuisine: avocados, chiles, chocolate, coconuts, corn, pumpkins, tomatoes and vanilla. The words chocolate and tomato are actually from the Aztec language. The array of food at the market was so enticing that it was hard to refuse, but refuse we must. Huge carcasses of beef were hung out in the open air, as were slaughtered pigs and chickens, with many flies and other insects hovering around and landing on each. Much of this meat was ultimately turned into the tacos, enchiladas, tamales, tostadas and the other tempting dishes sold "to go" from the stands at the market. The fresh fruits and vegetables looked absolutely luscious, but eating any of this would have probably meant we would be sick the next day. So we only ate a little of what Manuel considered would be safe for us.

There was so much to see that we kept drifting apart and Manuel had a difficult time keeping up with us. My food writer interests were aroused by a vendor selling a crudely-made metal gadget that he demonstrated by slicing and dicing, just like Ron Popeil and his Vege-Matic of American television fame. I, of course, just had to have one. Next to him was a vendor selling pottery bean pots which he cleverly hawked to us as "Mexican Corning Ware." Mariá was entranced by the baby Jesus dolls. A wide selection of clothes and accessories were sold for them and they proved to be extremely popular with the Indian children. Mariá couldn't resist, plus she also ended up buying a hand crocheted baby cap for her new grandchild and had quite a lively conversation in Spanish with the creator.

Adriana was in need of finding some inexpensive Mexican trinkets for her daughter Lynne to hand out as prizes to her pre-school Spanish students back in Minnesota. She found just what she needed and because she was buying in large quantity, she was able to bargain for a very reasonable price. We each bought t-shirts, handmade puzzles and other toys for all our grandchildren, without succumbing to what is known as the "sombrero syndrome." That is when you buy something as a souvenir that is completely out of place at home and is of absolutely no use to you either. In the end, none of us even bought a sombrero.

Joanna was inspired to purchase a small pottery "Circle of Friends," a grouping of four figures circling a candle holder in the center. The Indian legend says that at the end of the evening, friends would gather around a bonfire and share their hearts and speak of the good qualities of each other and remember times shared. As the embers faded, their friendship was said to be sealed anew, bringing them closer together. As you sit with the candle lit in the middle of your circle of friends, it will surround and embrace all who sit with you and bring good luck to those who stay together.

Once our shopping was completed, Manuel took us to see another highlight of Tepoztlán, the folk art at the Dominican Church. The gated entrance leading from the market to the churchyard is decorated with intricate patterns of corn kernels, black and red beans and sunflower seeds, reminiscent of the Corn Palace in South Dakota. Because we were visiting a church, it was then that Manuel chose to talk about our *ofrenda* for the day: SPIRITUALITY. "What I am referring to is not necessarily organized religion, but more the inspiration that we gain from all religions. True spirituality is complete acceptance, gratitude and forgiveness. Willpower alone is not enough to help any of us lead a worthy life. We also need God's energy and guidance, gained in whatever way we experience him. Even though I am Catholic,

I believe we still must study and learn from all religions.

"The cross, the outward symbol of my religion signifies renaissance or rebirth. The upright portion represents consciousness as a soaring bird reaching toward heaven. The cross beam represents the movement of time as a crawling serpent moves across the earth. The point at which they intersect in the middle signifies the here and now, where heaven and earth meet. The bird and the serpent become one as shown in the carvings of Quetzalcóatl, who, yet another legend portrays, planted a large wooden cross on the beach of Veracruz when he departed, which supposedly resisted all efforts to pull it down."

By now it was time for our late lunch and inside our restaurant, all of the interior walls were covered with a collection of magnificent Mexican masks. All manner of masks. There were eagles and jaguars, birds and reptiles and menacing deities who could bring abundant rain, fertile crops, successful harvests, and good health. Masks are folk art but to

Mexicans they mean much more than that. They are symbolic expressions that were used for defense, religious purposes or just for fun and entertainment. Masks were used to transform the wearer both physically and psychologically into gods, ferocious animals and supernatural forces. In this way the wearers, for a brief time, become whatever they choose. My favorite, by far, was the more handsome and gentle-looking Quetzalpapalotl Butterfly God mask.

During lunch, Manuel asked Joanna to tell us what specifically had brought her to Mexico. Joanna confessed that it was completely selfish on her part, that the butterflies were really the only reason she had come and that she had planned to simply endure all the other tours in order to finally have a chance to see the Monarchs she loved so much. Because she had spent many years working for Minnetonka Travel in Wayzata, she and Don were able to enjoy a great deal of travel together, but Don had no desire at all to see the butterflies. So when this opportunity arose, Joanna grabbed at the chance to go with us.

Joanna had the great good fortune of marrying her very best friend. They first met in high school and after graduation Joanna went off to see the world but finally came back to Wayzata to marry Don. Being social in those days always meant drinking, and drinking silently took its toll on Don. As they were experiencing the joys of becoming parents, the ever present drinking was adding stress. Although there was nothing horribly bad, the need to control every aspect of family life was taking its toll on Joanna. Don was a law enforcement officer and with Joanna's help, managed to hide his drinking problem and keep things looking fine on the outside, but on the inside life was less than satisfactory. One day, when he decided "there just had to be more to life than this" he went into treatment, and Joanna being the always supportive wife joined Al-anon.

At the time, she was "doing this for Don" and not for herself. She really didn't expect to get anything out of it personally. Joanna already thought she was quite capable of fixing just about anything or at least making it better, but eventually she grew to acknowledge her own co-dependent role. It was when she and Don both truly understood the healing spiritual meaning of letting go and letting God in the AA program, that life really became great for both of them, and they have spent many happy years together ever since, enjoying their family and friends and following their faith.

During this same time, Joanna was teaching a class for wives of new officers called "How to Live with the Law and Like It." She had once asked Don if he felt he needed to hide the fact that he had been in treatment, from his fellow law enforcement officers and he said no he didn't, but laughed that he often felt, however, that he needed to hide the fact that he was a cop from his fellow Alcoholics Anonymous members because in the past, they so often had so much trouble with the law.

The year 1976, when Don went into treatment, was coincidentally the very same year that the final destination of the migrating Monarchs was discovered in Mexico by researchers. Joanna read an article about this in a magazine and was obsessed with Monarchs from that time on. She read the article to all her family and friends and told them that someday her dream was to follow the Monarchs herself. Everyone humored her, but she never forgot. One spring when she and Don moved to their retirement home in western Minnesota, they were even welcomed by a whole yard covered with returning Monarchs who every year apparently appreciated stopping over to eat the abundance of purple phlox they found there plus the many evergreens in which to rest before moving on.

Joanna admitted that seeing the butterflies in Angangueo had finally completed the cycle begun for her by Al-Anon, that of releasing her own individual spirit, something just for her own needs. She also agreed that whenever she thought of herself being selfish, it always turned out for the best in the end for everyone concerned. Because Don was her best friend, she had never developed a group of close girlfriends and she considered the growing friendship among us to be a real gift to her.

As we left Tepoztlán, we were held up by an un-usual traffic jam, a large group of bulls being slowly led along the narrow street in front of us by their owner. When we finally reached the villa, the hot-tub was ready and Consuela had made *sopes* from our tortillas and cheese for a light supper. Manuel dropped us off and left because he had a church event to attend with his wife and daughter, but he reminded us that tomorrow we would be touring the sacred ruins of Xochicalco. We resumed our card competition, compared stories from back home, and Joanna lighted her Circle of Friends for us.

Xochicalco

Xochicalco means "in the place of the house of flowers." The six hundred acres of well-preserved ruins are located high on a hilltop overlooking a spacious valley less than thirty miles south of Cuernavaca. It is not known for sure who built them, but their peak period seems to have spanned the last phase of Teotihuacán. These uncrowded ruins offer an exceptional modern museum facility to those who make the trip. Manuel enjoyed using the laser pointer from his teaching days at the University to highlight on a giant-sized wall map the things that we shouldn't miss visiting. The most impressive would be the Temple of the Feathered

Serpent. It seems that every Mesoamerican society felt it had to have a temple honoring Quetzalcóatl, the feathered serpent, and this particular one featured flat sculptures of this diety stealthily slithering around all four sides.

Xochicalco was a much more serene place than Teotihuacán would prove to be. Here the people were encouraged to rest and improve themselves both mentally and physically. It was a fitness center with amenities unrivaled in their time. There was the standard oblong ball court in the shape of the letter I for playing *Tlachli,* a life and death religious game, common at the time, using a rubber ball to score through rings high up on the walls. The stakes were also high; those who lost were sometimes sacrificed. In addition, there was a large swimming pool and a very sophisticated steam bath, for it was felt that steam cleansed people both inside and out. Many secluded areas were in evidence apparently for relaxation and meditation. Leisure time seemed to be encouraged and the exchange of ideas highly valued. This was truly a place of well being.

While we walked about the ruins, Manuel discussed his *ofrenda* for the day: HEALING. "If you do not have good health, you have nothing. Natural healing seems to have had an important place here, as it still does even in our society today. Here you'll find an area that was especially devoted to an unusual ceremony involving an ancient healer utilizing only eggs. You may have noticed the many herbs and remedies for sale in the market at Tepoztlán. As a healer myself, I learned my craft from my Aztec ancestors and I use many of these natural remedies to help those in need. The Catholic healing influence has also been helpful for me. Remember the great importance given to the Virgin of Health in Pátzcuaro?

"I was once struck by lightning and when a person is struck by lightning and survives, as I did, he or she forever has the power to see and read auras, which helps to determine just what is wrong with a person and which remedy is necessary. There is, incidentally, a botanical garden and museum in Cuernavaca devoted to traditional medicinal herbs, and we will stop there briefly today if we get a chance. You will be amazed by all the effective natural remedies available for common ailments."

On our return to Cuernavaca, Manuel asked Mariá what had caused her to make this trip to Mexico. She didn't even have to give it a second thought. It was because Jerry had loved Mexico so much and she wanted to learn to speak Spanish to honor his memory and keep it alive. During their many years together, Mariá had never stopped having her heart skip a beat when Jerry entered the room. It was a wonderful romance that continued even through the many stresses of having six children. They had just absolutely adored one another.

In addition to being a very busy executive, the vice president of a company, Jerry was also a very dedicated father who was always there for his kids. The children were very close to their dad. The three oldest, all girls, were all married by that time and their dad's very sudden death took a huge toll. All three were so devastated that their marriages were unable to withstand the unrelenting emotional pain;

all three girls were divorced within a year of his death.

Jerry and Mariá had been anxiously awaiting, his early retirement, but Mariá planned to continue teaching, so she had told Jerry that when he retired, he would have to learn to cook. Mariá hated to cook and still does. Always the one to use humor to soften a difficult situation, she later told everyone in the family that she figured Jerry must not have liked the idea of cooking any better than she did, and decided death was a better alternative to having to learn to cook.

Before his death, with several kids in private colleges, and at a time when teaching jobs were in short supply, Mariá had decided that rather than simply lounging around or going out to lunch, she ought to do something more productive to bring in a little extra money, something temporary like house cleaning or waitressing. Without consulting Jerry, she went ahead and cleaned houses for a whole year before she confessed this to him. He was never embarrassed or upset by the many crazy things she did though, but was simply afraid that she might get fired because of her minimal housekeeping skills. He was, however, very happy for Mariá when she did get a job teaching again. Our group of friends was also a gift to Mariá. She had really remained in denial about Jerry's death for a long time, and she admitted to us that it wasn't until our trip that she finally was able to say the words "my husband died."

As we neared the outskirts of Cuernavaca, we approached a cemetery that still had remnants of decorations from the Day of the Dead on the 2nd of November. Mexican cemeteries are especially colorful and creative just as they are, but that all changes even for the better at the end of October each year. Manuel stopped for a few minutes to describe this national holiday to us. "Preparations begin at just the exact time the Monarch butterflies begin returning to Mexico. Mexicans believe that these are the returning souls of their deceased family and friends. This is not a sad time, but rather, is a time for celebration. My people believe that we are not here for a long time, but we are here to have a happy time, and that those who fear death don't enjoy life. Death is considered as just one more inevitable phase in the continuing cycle of life.

"On the Day of the Dead, the souls of all we hold dear return to visit and comfort us. They are here for us, but we are also here for them. An altar is prepared either at home or at the cemetery to welcome them. A picture of those being honored guides them to us, and to where the spirits will find all their favorite foods, drink, and sometimes costumes and amusements. In addition they'll find many marigolds and other bright flowers, candles, sugar candy skulls and skeletons, chocolates and even a special bread, *Pan de Muertos*. When these gifts are offered, the family gathers and the vigil begins either in the home with a feast or at the cemetery with a midnight picnic.

"This ancient celebration now incorporates the best of Aztec customs and Catholic All Saints and All Souls days. The Day of the Dead also happens to fall at the same time as Halloween and seems somewhat similar with the costumes, candy, ghosts and skeletons, but unlike Halloween, it is not considered frightening at all. It is a festive celebration. Mariá, we know you saw a Monarch butterfly heading toward heaven when you got the news that Jerry had died. This was undoubtedly his soul telling you in a Mexican way that he was in good hands and that he would always be there for you."

On our way home, we stopped for a late lunch at another Cuernavaca landmark, *Hacienda de Cortés*, one of the most important sugar mills of the colonial era. This once grand home of Hernán Cortés was destroyed during the Mexican revolution. It was ultimately renovated and now serves as a hotel with lovely gardens and a restaurant with an international menu. Many of the stone walls have amate roots growing right out of them in an unbelievable tangle which could certainly tell many tales from earlier times.

Next we stopped to visit the Spanish Immersion Language School where Mariá would be spending the two weeks following our return to Minnesota.

We were then sent on our way to visit with Esperanza, the mother who would be taking Mariá under her roof and her wing to live with her family, speaking only Spanish for those two weeks. By then we were unfortunately too late to see the herb museum. Maybe another day.

At our villa, Mariá, Adriana and I talked with Paco in English, while Manuel applied a healing ointment to a chronically painful spot on Joanna's ankle. She reported that it did give her some immediate relief. Carmen's handsome son, Omar, stopped by to visit with Adriana. Omar is working toward becoming a golf pro in Mexico and Jack had brought him to Minnesota for several summers to assist him, and to live in their home.

When we told Omar we would be going to the National Museum of Anthropology in Mexico City the next day, he couldn't believe it, and asked us why we would want to do such a thing. He told us he seldom went to Mexico City and always took his revolver along when he did, and that we should be sure to do the same. Manuel said he would definitely be taking "The Club," a device which securely locks his steering wheel in place, at which Omar laughed and said that he also takes "the club," his nine iron, which, if necessary, can be a very effective weapon.

That evening, we had our final dip in the hot tub because our last two days of touring would be much too busy for that. We finished up all the homemade salsa and guacamole while we completed our three-day card competition. Joanna, who had once again lighted her Circle of Friends in our honor, was the big winner—a grand total of $13. Tomorrow we would plan to arrive in Mexico City just as their famous morning rush hour gridlock subsided.

Mexico City

It was the gun that woke us once again. Actually it was the lack of a gun. The gun was missing; we asked Consuela and Magdelana and none of us could find the missing gun anywhere. It had completely disappeared! Manuel was concerned to hear this and was very unhappy not to have this added insurance for our safety after Omar's words of caution.

During our ride from Cuernavaca, Manuel explained that our *ofrenda* for the day was HISTORY, and that we would certainly see why when we arrived at the museum, where history would speak for itself. "The gift of history, just like the gift of myth, gives us a real feeling for who we are and we learn to appreciate all we have gained from the past. Because history so often repeats itself, hopefully knowing this prevents us from making at least some of the same mistakes all over again. Carefully preserving and understanding history is one of the best indications of an enlightened society and goes a long way toward creating peace and helping to prevent future wars."

Mexico City, still considered one of the largest cities in the world, is famous for both its relentless smog and its rush hour traffic, which never seems to end. Manuel was very familiar with getting around the city, and we were even able to pass slowly by several large and extravagant homes that he had designed. He had carefully picked his route to Chapultepec Park, the location of the Mexican National Museum of Anthropology. Our plan to avoid rush hour traffic was a good one because what little traffic remained, still seemed quite heavy to our Midwestern traffic sensibilities.

Mariá pointed out a dilapidated turquoise pick-up truck that had been behind us since we neared the city. The truck, with two young Mexican men in the front, was quite an amusing sight. It looked like it had been dunked into a big vat of turquoise paint, dents and all, and the many drips had just dried where they were. It appeared to be a Ford or Chevy, but hard to tell since everything except the tires was covered in turquoise paint. As we arrived at the museum, the pick-up truck turned away.

There was a large crowd gathered in the park outside the museum. Here were the Aztec *Voladores*, the flying dancers from Veracruz, who attempted to imitate the flight of the gods. Four men, dressed as birds, at the top of a high tower, with ropes wound around their waists, jumped headfirst like bungee jumpers toward the ground, while a fifth man stayed on a platform at the top and played haunting flute music. The tower slowly spun around thirteen times as the ropes unwound and the men "flew" toward earth. It was kind of like a maypole ceremony in reverse, but considerably more dangerous. When all four men completed their thirteen circles and landed upright on their feet, they had together completed 52 cycles, which is symbolic of the Aztec "bundle of years." This ancient religious ceremony is thought to connect heaven and earth, past and present. The Voladores really brought history to life for us. Manuel's only comment was: "That's AMAZING!"

As we entered what is considered to be one of the best museums in the world, we were greeted by the Mexican flag, consisting of three wide vertical stripes: green for independence, white for religion, and red for union. In the center of the white stripe is the coat of arms, showing an enormous eagle with a snake in its beak and talons, standing on a prickly-pear cactus. The flag honors the legend that Mexico City was built on the site where the Aztecs encountered the long predicted eagle, snake and cactus. Mexicans celebrate their flag on national holidays by replicating the colors with a special dish, *chiles en nogada*, made of stuffed green chiles covered in a thick white sauce, then sprinkled with bright red pomegranate seeds.

I had spent some time before our trip reading about Mexican history and the many amazing artifacts that had been discovered throughout the years. I was awestruck to see so many of them in person, collected together all in one space, especially the famous Aztec Calendar Stone and the monumental sculptures of many gods and goddesses such as Tlaloc and Chalchicutlicue, god and goddess of rain, and Huehuctlotl, god of fire.

The Aztec Calendar Stone, or Stone of the Sun, is a gigantic carved disc weighing twenty-four tons that depicts the whole of Aztec history. The Aztecs saw time as being circular, like an endlessly turning wheel. They actually used two intersecting calendar wheels, the sacred one for planning religious festivals (260 days) and the other, the solar wheel, for measuring the seasons and the times for planting and harvesting (365 days). Both made use of the number thirteen. The 260-day sacred cycle was divided into twenty months of thirteen days, each with their own name and number. The 365-day solar cycle was divided into four seasons of thirteen weeks. These cycles acted like the turning of two differently sized gears with the first day of the 260 - day calendar and the first day of the 365-day calendar arriving at the very same point only once every 52 years. A new century began at this time with the ceremonial burning of the bundling of the years.

It was believed that the gods created the sun five different times. The Aztec Calendar Stone shows these five suns. The first four were ultimately destroyed along with the whole world by natural disasters brought on by the gods. The fifth sun, in which we are still in now, is predicted to be destroyed by earthquakes. This was the frightening thought that kept the ancient Aztecs providing blood sacrifices to their gods. They believed the gods sacrificed themselves in the beginning in order for humans to live and so it was necessary to repay the gods for their selfless acts, in order to keep the world from being destroyed again. Seems like it worked, the world is still here.

The Aztecs also believed the earth was a flat disc surrounded by water. Above the disc was heaven, consisting of thirteen layers and underneath was the underworld made up of nine layers. When you died, somewhere in all of these layers you found your destination for your afterlife depending on how deserving your life had been.

After we completed our tour of the museum, we stopped in the gift shop and, surprisingly, I found an attractive coffee table book about Quetzalcóatl in English, entitled, "Legends of the Plumed Serpent," the exact same book that I had recently purchased for myself at The Bookcase, my cozy little independent bookstore in Wayzata. All of us agreed that this book would make a perfect thank-you gift for Manuel when we said our final farewell in just two more days.

In order for us to wait out the evening rush hour, but enable us to get on the road well before dark, we decided to grab a very quick and early dinner at, of all places, McDonald's. Always predictable when you need food fast, a Big Mac, is a Big Mac, is a Big Mac. Besides, I do own just a little McDonald's stock, so it's always fun to check out how they are doing in another country. Once we were on the road again, it was now my turn. Manuel wanted to know what it was that had brought me to Mexico and the butterflies.

When I was in high school in McLean, Virginia, outside of Washington, DC, my simple summer job was preserving insects at the Smithsonian. To me, the big black beetles and bugs were frightening and ugly, but the beautiful butterflies captured my heart and my imagination. When much later I learned that the Monarchs gathered to winter in Mexico, I wanted to visit them, but at the time, my marriage was falling apart, and a trip to Mexico just wasn't in the picture.

When Dan and I married, we truly thought we were in love, but it seems we were actually follow-ing a carefully created script of the Sixties: graduate from college, get a good job, get married, buy a nice house and have several children. When we married, we had only known each other for six months. Our basic values were somewhat the same, but we found our goals and interests were not similar at all.

Through the many trials that life threw at us, it was almost inevitable and certainly merciful that we should split apart.

It was the death of the dream, or rather what the script said should be the dream, that was so hard to accept. In thirty years, for better or worse, we had created our own family history, for us and for our children. We both strongly believed that marriage should be for life, but when you think you know the person you are marrying, and you both turn out to be totally different from what you thought, you have in effect married a stranger. Unfortunately it turned out that neither of us had married the best friend and soul mate that we had hoped for.

The tearing apart, whether welcome or not, of thirty years spent going through the motions of a marriage together, creates a lot of hate, anger and turmoil. Forgiveness and time are the only cures that can create the magic of healing. Now that the years have passed, I can say that Dan and I have a much greater appreciation for the things that we did love about one another and we are able to mostly overlook the things we hated. We are much better friends now and are much happier than we ever were when we were married. As we have learned this week, the Aztecs believed death is simply a re-birth, and in the end, so is divorce.

Just a few weeks before the trip, I celebrated my 60th birthday and a week before that, the world celebrated the arrival of the new millennium. For so many reasons in my life, I have always felt a compelling desire to travel in Mexico. In my own Midwestern surroundings I was always drawn toward Mexico's vivid colors and crafts, to the point of using them to decorate in my stucco home, which reminded me of a hacienda. Could I have been a sultry señorita in another life? I also cooked many marvelous Mexican meals for my family and friends, who, upon seeing my collection of bulls and bull-fighters, commented that they had always had a feeling I was "full of bull," actually not a bad trait for a writer. My new-found freedom was what has allowed me to make this exciting trip and the butterflies were indeed the belated icing on my 60th birthday cake.

We managed to avoid the evening rush hour and we didn't need the gun after all. Manuel deposited us at the villa, and we immediately dropped into bed, but we all had trouble sleeping in anticipation of seeing Teotihuacán and learning the message the next day.

Teotihuacán

After a fairly uneventful day yesterday, when even the smog was tolerable, today was already becoming alarming. Two things would happen simultaneously that would cause us concern. Manuel had mapped out what he felt was the easiest and safest route to Teotihuacán. Our route would by necessity take us right through Mexico City again, so he had once again timed our arrival to avoid the worst of the morning rush hour. Not long after we finally entered the city, however, we were stopped by a blockade of police cars with wildly flashing lights and many policemen, with guns drawn. We learned that protestors had forcibly captured control of the university and so after being searched, we were rerouted to a detour unfamiliar to Manuel. We could tell that he was nervous about this, especially since we had no gun of our own, but we continued to work our way through the gridlock.

At about the same time, Mariá mentioned that the turquoise pick-up truck with the same two young men from yesterday, had been following us again since we entered Mexico City. She felt there was absolutely no doubt they were following us, because the truck continued right behind us even on the detour and followed us all the way to the parking lot at Teotihuacán. Joanna managed to get some good video of the pick-up and the young men in the front seat. Once we entered the ruins, they turned and quickly headed in the opposite direction.

Manuel explained that Xochicalco, a place of well being, was merely a prelude to Teotihuacán, a place of imagination. Manuel's idol, Frank Lloyd Wright, had even visited these same ruins for inspiration. All of these ancient sacred sites and their positive energy are a tangible reminder that the whole world will one day be awakening to a more peaceful place. Rediscovered by the Aztecs, it is not known who built Teotihuacán or what caused it to be abandoned, perhaps drought, invasion or internal turmoil.

Try to picture the great green grassy mall in Washington, D.C, which stretches from the Capitol to the Washington Monument, but instead of grass, envision a wide, mile-long, stone-paved avenue called The Avenue of the Dead, and instead of impressive government buildings, great museums and magnificent monuments, see many Mesoamerican temples, palaces and pyramids lining the way on each side. This is the magnitude of Teotihuacán, the City of the Gods. Built more than two thousand years ago, it covers nearly eight square miles, much of which has yet to be excavated.

Volumes have been written describing this ancient city, but in brief, we began with the Citadel, a very large square or parade ground, larger than thirty football fields, located at one end of The Avenue of the Dead. We were immediately surrounded by Indians, playing eerie music on pottery whistles, which they were hoping to sell to us as souvenirs. The dust and dirt in the square were constantly whipped up by the wind into little cyclones called "dust devils." As we approached the Temple of Quezalcóatl, located within the Citadel, I reasoned that since Quetzalcóatl was the god of the wind, then these wind-driven "dust devils" must be his ghost welcoming us. The imposing open-mouthed sculptures of the head of Quetzalcóatl, jutting way out from the sides of the temple, allowed those who so chose to insert their arm into the mouth cavity all the way up to their arm pit, as demonstrated by Adriana.

Halfway down The Avenue of the Dead is the tallest structure, the towering Pyramid of the Sun. On the far end is the slightly smaller, but still mammoth, Pyramid of the Moon. Pyramids were built to bring humans closer to heaven, and these certainly have succeeded. Both of these pyramids can be climbed by those who are brave enough, but the steps are incredibly steep and those afraid of heights would want to think twice. We all chose to just enjoy the view of the Pyramid of the Sun from below, but Adriana, Joanna, Mariá and Manuel decided to climb the somewhat easier Pyramid of the Moon. Being afraid of heights myself, I watched from the safety of the solid ground below. When they returned, Mariá reported that from above she had noticed the two young men from the pick-up truck hanging around in front of the Palace of the Quetzalpapalotl God, located right next to the Pyramid of the Moon.

The Butterfly God, as this handsome deity is also known, is a combination of the *quetzal* (bird) and the *papalotl* (butterfly). The palace is adorned with thick stone pillars decorated with giant sentry-sized sculptures of the Butterfly God. Their large, round eyes are inlaid with coal black obsidian, the mirror-like, hard stone that was treasured by the Aztecs for making weapons. Right here in this courtyard was where we were to receive the message just a little later that day. Manuel told us that our instruction was to linger there in the shadows just at closing. It had been arranged that when all the other visitors were gone, an Aztec priest would appear to present us with the message.

Covering everything in Teotihuacán takes more than a day, so we were only able to hit the highlights, but this was certainly enough to satisfy us. Manuel had made many visits to Teotihuacán, and he wanted us to see the nearby ruins of Atetelco, the massive complex of apartments built for the ancient Indian workers of Teotihuacán. We laughed when we saw a sign as we entered that said in Spanish, "High Heels Prohibited," as if anyone would even consider wearing anything but their most comfortable walking shoes at a place like this. It was here that we were able to see amazing examples of recently restored murals of ferocious wild animals. The vivid colors just jumped out at us, and the blood red background made the animals impossible to ignore.

Now we were tired and hungry and it was still too early for the ruins to close, so we went across the highway to visit a different type of tourist attraction, Pyramid Charlie's, where the amusing sign promised "the food made great by the Aztecs." After our McDonalds the night before, we were again craving some authentic Mexican food and weren't disappointed. In addition, we each washed down our dinner with a huge bowl-sized margarita to take the edge off the suspense which was rapidly building.

As it neared closing time at the ruins, we headed back toward the Palace of the Butterfly God. Only three people were there when we arrived in the main courtyard. They soon left together and there we were, alone at last, ready to receive our Aztec priest. The priest appeared right on time, looking very ancient and wise in his long black robes, and he acknowledged Manuel with a nod. He carried a football-sized container, a clay replica of a cocoon or chrysalis that was heavily embellished with shimmering gold. He explained to Manuel that an amate paper scroll bearing the message was inside, and was written in Nahuatl, which Manuel would have to translate for us. As he was about to twist off the top and remove the message, two tall male figures appeared from the shadows, one with a handgun pointed right at us and the other blocking our escape. They demanded that the chrysalis containing the message be handed to them. These were the same two young men who had been following us. The priest reluctantly handed over the coveted prize and the men quickly melted back into the shadows.

After wailing a very loud and haunting lament, the priest also disappeared into the shadows. We were absolutely shocked, and it took a few minutes for us to collect ourselves. We exited the ruins as quickly as possible, encountering an armed guard at the front entrance, where we had parked our van. We were glad to see him, but there was nothing we could say or do. How could we ever explain this? All we could do was return, empty handed, to the safety of our villa, first through the unfamiliar streets of Mexico City and then through the dark mountains to Cuernavaca. We silently prayed for a safe return while Manuel drove on, tightly clasping his St. Christopher's medal. No one followed us this time.

Greta, our guard dog, greeted us at the door and we all sat on the patio, stunned and saddened by what had happened. What was the meaning of all of this? How could anyone have known our plans? Manuel was bemoaning the fact that he had almost had the ancient words right in his hands, but now we would be leaving tomorrow without any of us ever knowing what the scroll said.

Suddenly, we heard a male voice calling to us: "*Señor!,..... Señoras!*" We looked up to see a small male figure holding a handgun. His face was covered with a mask that resembled the Quetzal-paplotl, the Butterfly God. How had he gotten in? Why hadn't Greta barked and protected us? The masked gunman put down his gun and removed his disguise. It was Paco and he was talking very rapidly in Spanish to Manuel, who didn't seem at all threatened. Greta knew Paco well, so of course she wouldn't have barked when he entered the villa.

Manuel explained that the men who had taken the chrysalis from us were Paco's cousins. They meant us no harm, but they desired to retrieve and retain the chrysalis for future Aztec generations. The Spanish had already taken most of the gold from the Aztecs and the chrysalis was a valuable artifact, a remnant of that gold which they felt should always be preserved for them. They knew that the misguided and somewhat greedy priest only wanted to keep this valuable artifact for himself and they just couldn't let that happen. The gold-encrusted chrysalis should forever continue to be the sacred container for the many future generations awaiting messages from their Aztec ancestors.

Paco told us in English that he had been watching us closely in Cuernavaca since our first day at the cathedral, and that his job of listening to us and reporting our plans to his cousins, and "borrowing" our gun, was now complete. So he would now leave, never to return to the villa again. He handed Manuel the handgun, minus the bullets, plus the amate paper message, which he said was indeed meant for all of us. With this, he picked up his mask, another valuable Aztec artifact that he had worn especially to give him courage, and left by the back entrance to the pool.

Manuel quickly unrolled the scroll and read it to himself and then translated the Nahuatl into English for us. "At the change of the Millennium, on our continent, a critical mass of people, who have lived half a century or more, will have been established. This group will continue to grow larger day by day. Many of these wise and experienced individuals will genuinely wish to finally discover their true purpose in life. These are the enlightened ones, those who have the desire to fully experience their own individual gifts. They will share these gifts with those they love in order to make the world a better and more peaceful place. Everyone on earth has a special God-given gift or purpose, a reason for being. Your years after fifty are God's special GIFT OF GOLD to you, your golden years. This gift is your *ofrenda* for today and every day for the rest of your lives, a time to pursue your true talents and passions and give the result away."

Manuel realized that we would each find true Aztec gold, not in the cold, hard metal that had been the cause of so many wars, but in our own golden years. He reminded us that there is really nothing new in the universe, it is just that each generation needs to rediscover these lessons for itself. His *ofrendas* had really only been reminders of information that we each already possessed, the sum total of which serves to enhance our "gift of gold." Except for a very few wise elders, it was only very recently that much of mankind has managed to live beyond the age of fifty. Now with these added years, it is our chance to take up the challenge of wise elderhood, just like the golden Monarch butterfly emerging from the cocoon.

"These wonderful years after fifty are first and foremost for having fun and relaxing because we have earned and deserve this. But somewhere between sitting in an RV or a golf cart and a rocking chair or wheelchair there is the important job of giving your gift back to the world. The price of not pursuing your true passion or purpose during these years is boredom, lethargy, depression and ultimately ill health and even an earlier death.

"When we are young we are busy raising families and making our mark in the world, we often don't have time to discover who we really are, but when we finally do have the time to reflect, our gifts can be unearthed by focusing on what it is that we truly have a passion for doing. These gifts can be as grand as contributing a large amount of money to a worthy cause or leading a movement for peace and social improvement, to as simple as volunteering to spend our time helping those in need, or cooking, sewing, gardening or woodworking and sharing the results with family and friends."

We still were not quite sure why we specifically were chosen to receive this message, but Manuel assured us that he would explain this to us the next day on our way to the airport. We were ready to try to understand and tackle the challenge, but not just at this very moment. First we needed the soothing renewal of sleep. It had been a very long, confusing, and stress filled day. Manuel left us and once again we dropped into bed.

Mexico City

Morning came all too soon. Had we really slept? Had yesterday all been just a dream? No, this had all been very real and Manuel would be arriving sometime before noon to take us to the airport, so we rapidly and reluctantly packed for our return to Minnesota. Then we each wrote a special message in the gift book we had purchased for Manuel at the museum store.

When Manuel finally arrived, he joined us for coffee and Mexican pastries. He had typed up an English translation of the Aztec message, and he had cut the original amate paper scroll into five equal strips, one for each of us, including himself, so that we would each possess and always be a part of the whole. He had also brought four identical thin silver wire chokers that he had designed and made as his gift for us, using the silver and stones he had purchased at the market in Taxco. There was a silver cross in the middle of each with a grouping of thirteen bright red stones on either side of the cross.

We were quite touched and asked him what the design symbolized. The circular choker symbolized our circle of friends and the continuous nature of our never-ending friendship. The cross signified the spiritual blending of our past, present and future. The color red signified the bonding nature of our blood and the thirteen stones signified the thirteen days we had spent together in the land of the Aztec, the equivalent of exactly one Aztec sacred month. Manuel noted we had previously seen that the number thirteen is quite prominent in the Aztec culture and is not thought of as being unlucky at all, as it is to so many Americans.

We presented Manuel with the signed book and he, too, was very touched to know that we considered him such a special friend. It was now noon and time to load up the van for our last and final trip to Mexico City. Mariá would ride along and then return with Manuel to Cuernavaca for her two weeks of intensive Spanish lessons. Manuel told us that we had already shared our final *ofrenda*, the gift of FRIENDSHIP, "a gift which you have so generously given to me and to yourselves. You took a big risk on each other and on me and look how well it all turned out. In the end, the danger in making this trip was ultimately much less than the danger of staying at home and never having experienced any of this."

During the drive to Mexico City, Manuel, as promised, began explaining why we were chosen to be given the Aztec message. He began by listing for us, one by one, the qualities he saw in each of us that would enable us to perpetuate the Gift of Gold:

"Adriana, the Organizer, disciplined, loving, giving, a thoughtful, fun filled friend."

"Joanna, the Promoter, speaker, supporter, a kind listener, has never met a stranger."

"Mariá, the Educator, adventurer, free spirit, humorous, loves to teach and learn."

"Miki, the Creator, writer, dreamer, instigator, always thinking we need to try this."

Manuel summed us up by saying "you all have a wonderful, curious, open-minded, non-judgmental quality in common. I basically see you as ready for anything that isn't illegal, immoral or indecent, and even then, if necessary you might sometimes slightly push the envelope. You are ordinary women, yet each of you have special talents that will help encourage others to give their Gift of Gold to the world. Just as the magnificent Monarch who connects the continent, you each have the ability to help connect many people with this message.

"Crisis is a duality from which you can choose to either grow or perish. The wisdom you have gained through successfully surviving a major crisis in your own lives and then thriving in your golden years make you especially inspiring to others. It was the universe that arranged to have all of our paths meet in Mexico. Now, I hope you understand why you were chosen. Quetzalcóatl and his wise and gentle ways can now be reborn through each of you every day, bringing only peace, love and butterflies.

Just before we headed to the gate, I asked Manuel to tell us why he had come on this adventure with us. "I didn't fully know the answer to that question until yesterday at Teotihuacán," he said. Because of such a poor economy in Mexico, I have suffered a rather forced and reluctant retirement from both teaching and designing homes, and I saw this as a great opportunity to earn a few extra pesos and possibly have a meaningful adventure for myself. It was after I accepted this job that I was told by my wise elders about the message and given my additional assignment of connecting with all of you, so that we could all discover the message together. As a person also in my golden years, I will be watching with great interest to see what good work you do with this information, and attempt to do the same myself."

As we walked away to board our plane, we looked back over the waiting crowd and we couldn't miss the face of our guide. His infectious grin lit up the whole room with the warmth and intensity of the mid-day Mexican sun.

Epilogue

Here is an update of what has happened in our lives in the five years since our trip and the publication of this book. I think that Manuel would approve and be very pleased with what we have done to give the Gift of Gold.

Adrienne and Jack have celebrated their 42nd anniversary, and now have five grandchildren who live close by and enjoy sharing in their daily activities. They continue to sponsor a child in the orphanage, *Nuestros Pequeños Hermanos*. Adrienne has volunteered teaching English as a second language. She serves as the events chair for Friends of *Niños Adelante*, a non-profit educational program for the needy children of Zihuatanejo/Ixtapa, Mexico, and she and Jack have continued to make several trips to Mexico each year. She has helped to make many quilts for charity and also helped Miki conduct a grandmother/granddaughter tea party event for community education. Most recently, she has returned from a trip to China and is looking forward to a trip to Kenya, Africa in January 2005. Adrienne says she has relinquished control and has let others plan these trips, but she would still like to organize another trip to Mexico for the "feisty four."

Jo Ann and Don have celebrated their 41st anniversary and continue to enjoy entertaining their four grandchildren, especially during their annual "cousin camp." Jo Ann volunteers weekly at the Senior Nutrition Center/Meals on Wheels, quarterly at the Red Cross mobile blood drive, serves as treasurer for the community club, and is a past president of the local community garden club. In honor of her father and father-in-law, who both lost the battle to cancer, she acts as an area team captain for the annual American Cancer Society Relay for Life Team. During this time, Don was diagnosed with prostate cancer and she supported him through his treatment and he is now considered a cancer survivor. Jo Ann continues to accept speaking engagements on behalf of families of those in recovery from alcoholism. Her travels have taken her to China and on a Mediterranean cruise that included Spain, France, Italy, Greece, and Croatia.

Beryl Marie, who had been married almost thirty years before tragedy struck, managed to successfully raise her six children and see that they all received a college education. Now she is very involved with her seven grandchildren. Beryl has worked as a substitute teacher and has registered immigrant children for the school district. She has also taught English as a second language as a volunteer with Adrienne. In addition, she even helped a friend in California who is a third-grade teacher, by assisting her for three weeks to teach her Spanish-speaking third graders. Since our trip, Beryl has managed to fulfill a lifelong dream of living on a lake. She continues improving her Spanish-speaking skills and keeps up a steady e-mail correspondence with her many new friends in Mexico. She has returned to Mexico three times, and has also been to Spain and Greece.

I have spent these past five years periodically working on this book, and then finally seeing it to completion. I now have four grandchildren whom I have the pleasure of seeing each and every day, because we all live under the same roof. In the interim, my father needed my care and so I spent several years attending to his needs until he passed away at the age of ninety-two. In addition I have continued on the board of directors of Ageless Possibilities, a non-profit organization that promotes the creation of multi-generational housing. I have also volunteered on occasional projects with community education, Interfaith Outreach and the Minnetonka Center for the Arts. Some of the proceeds from the sale of this book will be given to Minnesota Friends of *Nuestros Pequeños Hermanos*, the Monarch Butterfly Sanctuary Foundation and the Hennepin County Library Foundation. My recent travels have taken me to France and Puerta Vallerta, Mexico, and I am looking forward to Adrienne getting "back in the saddle again" and planning another trip to Mexico for us.

As a synchronistic sidenote, soon after our return from Mexico, the Monarch Butterfly was proclaimed by the State of Minnesota as the official state butterfly.

About the Author

Known throughout the Midwest for her tireless creativity and enthusiasm, Miki Banavige often appeared around her hometown of Minneapolis cooking up new creations. She is the well-known author of *Cooking is M.A.G.I.C. (Making Any Groceries into Cuisine)* and *Hooked on Salmon*. Miki is now ready to get out of the frying pan and into the fire of creative non-fiction.

If you'd like to contact the author, she can be reached through the publisher or by email at miki@findingaztecgold.com. She'd love to hear from you.

Acknowledgments

A special thanks to those who helped make this book a reality: Kira Henschel, Goblin Fern Press; Wendy Johnson, Cover Designer; Scott Edelstein, Writing and Publishing Consultant; Sharon Magnuson, Computer Consultant and Web Sight Designer; Brian Bellmont, Publicist; The Loft Literary Center, Open U-The Learning Annex, Hennepin County Libraries, Villa Maria Retreat and Conference Center, and especially to all my many wonderful writing instructors, family and friends who supported my dream.

Order Form

To order your copy of **Finding Aztec Gold** by Miki Banavige, please fill out the following information.

Name

Address

City   State   Zip

Email

Phone

Method of Payment:

☐ Check

☐ Money Order

☐ Visa   ☐ MasterCard   ☐ AMEX

Credit Card #

Signature

Quantity: _____ x $12.95: _____

Minus discount* of: _____

S & H : _____

Subtotal: _____

If ordering from Wisconsin, please add 5.5% sales tax: _____

Order total: _____

Shipping and Handling:

$4.00 for 1st book, $1 per book thereafter. Unless otherwise requested, books will be sent

*Quantity Discount:
10% when ordering more than 20 books.

Exp. date

Please copy this order form and send or fax with payment to:

Goblin Fern Press

3809 Mineral Point Road
Madison, WI 53705
Phone: 608-442-0212 / Fax: 608-442-0221
Toll-free: 888-670-BOOK (2665)
Email: info@goblinfernpress.com

Or order from our secure website: www.GoblinFernPress.com

AGBK